Contents

A–Z

OF

ABERDEEN

PLACES - PEOPLE - HISTORY

Lorna Corall Dey

AMBERLEY

First published 2019

Amberley Publishing
The Hill, Stroud, Gloucestershire, GL5 4EP
www.amberley-books.com

Copyright © Lorna Corall Dey, 2019

The right of Lorna Corall Dey to be identified
as the Author of this work has been asserted in
accordance with the Copyrights, Designs and
Patents Act 1988.

ISBN 978 1 4456 8517 5 (print)
ISBN 978 1 4456 8518 2 (ebook)

British Library Cataloguing in Publication Data
A catalogue record for this book is available
from the British Library.

Origination by Amberley Publishing.
Printed in Great Britain.

Introduction

Latitude 57° north and longitude -2° west, 3,654 km from the North Pole, average annual rainfall 814.9 mm (around half Scotland's average of 1,570.9 mm), average annual hours of sunshine 1,435.7 (over 250 hours above the Scottish average), Aberdeen sits between two rivers, the Dee and Don, both flowing beneath ancient bridges before spilling out into the North Sea.

The *auld braif toun o' Bon-Accord* was once four districts – Crooked, Even, Futtie and Green – sharing among them crowded closes, pends and nooks such as Galens Close, Mitchell's Court, Shuttle Lane, Garden Nook Close, Donald's Court, Wordie's Pend, Rotten Raw, Huckster Wynd, and Round Table.

Aberdeen, regional capital of the north-east – the Granite City, the Silver City by the Golden Sands, the Oil Capital of Europe and, to the ancient Greeks and Romans, Devana. Ptolemy of Alexandria on his second-century globe showed Devana alongside the River Diva (Dee) inhabited by Texaloi peoples of Caledonia. Aberdeen, Aberdon, Aberdene, Aberden (the prefix Aber signifying river mouth); to most native-born it is Aiberdeen.

Ten centuries after Ptolemy, King David I made Aberdeen a royal burgh and William I, William the Lion, in the late 1100s granted Aberdeen's merchants and craftsmen 'their free Hanse' – their passport to travel and trade. Commerce prospered through 'extensive foreign trade', especially with the Low Countries, northern France and Hanseatic League towns.

Aberdeen, regarded as isolated within Scotland, has nevertheless enjoyed a thousand years of trading with the world. The first transatlantic voyage from Scotland was the *William* out of Aberdeen, in 1596. While Aberdeen's considerable contribution to Scotland's and Britain's economies has tended to be underrated, Sir Patrick

View of Aberdeen from above the Chain Briggie.

Looking westward along Union Street from the Castlegate.

Drummond, a seventeenth-century conservator in Holland, noted that merchandise from Aberdeen returned more from its trade than all the other towns in Scotland.

Aberdeen's first lighthouse was a large lamp attached to a wall on St Ninian's Chapel at Castlehill in 1566 – the 'gryt bowat' was visible to harbour-bound vessels. For its role during the Wars of Independence including regaining the town's *faire castell*, Aberdeen was rewarded with land by King Robert the Bruce – the start of the Common Good Fund to boost town assets, an unusual honour and the first such granted to a burgh.

Parson Gordon's 1661 map, *Abredonia Vetus, the Old towne of Aberdone*, shows a town of houses large and small, gardens, meandering streets, churches, a university, mills, friaries, loch and harbour all protected by five gates or ports – Footdee, Netherkirkgate, Overkirkgate, Gallowgate and Justice Port at Porthill. Porthill gate, Aberdeen Castle and St Katherine's Hill chapel are represented as three towers in Aberdeen's coat of arms encased within a double tressure decorated with fleurs-de-lis. (A double tressure was granted in recognition of Aberdeen's part in the Wars of Independence.) The city leopards are there and its motto, *Bon-Accord*. The back of the coat of arms shows St Nicholas (Niclaus, patron saint of Aberdeen), children and mariners under a porch pointing heavenward while praying over three children being boiled in a cauldron. According to legend he refused to eat what he recognised as human flesh and his prayers restored the children to life. Aberdeen's principal church, St Nicholas, is the Mither Kirk.

CASTLE STREET, ABERDEEN.

Cassie laying and carriages for hire.

Aberdeen was Scotland's only town to reject the National Covenant of 1638 and as a consequence came under attack from Montrose's Covenanting army at the Battle of the Brig o' Dee. The principal of Catholic King's College was replaced by Dr William Gauld, himself ousted by General Monk's troops during further religious purges under Cromwell's regime.

Young men from the north headed to Aberdeen for their education. Aberdeen Grammar School, established around 1257, is one of Britain's oldest schools. By the end of the sixteenth century, and unique in the British Isles, Aberdeen possessed two universities, matching England's total. The city's first printing press was set up in 1623 by Edward Raban and in 1748 Aberdeen produced its first newspaper, the *Aberdeen Journal*.

Changes to the town came thick and fast. The harbour, merchants and commerce were its lifeblood and boosted a host of trades and industries including shipbuilding, fishing, granite, combs, paper, woollen trades, chemicals and engineering.

> Thro' the braif toon where'er you look,
> For stirring sights there's never loss,
> Frae cleave-the-win' to Poynernook,
> Frae Rub'slaw to the Market Cross!

We will meet with some of Cadenhead's *stirring sights* in the course of this book, but such a brief A–Z of a city with as long and illustrious a history as Aberdeen is a near-impossible task. This is my A–Z; another volume could look quite different.

Aberdeen Sands

The tune *The Lang Sands o' Aberdeen* was inspired by the best beach in Scotland – a 2-mile stretch of golden sand from Don-mouth to Dee-mouth that is prevented from blowing away by a series of wooden groins extending into the North Sea.

No longer the draw it was since foreign holidays offered warmer options for dookers and sunbathers, the beach is a magnet for walkers, joggers, surfers, golfers, cyclists and for the less energetic there are restaurants, cinemas and an amusement park.

Particularly hardy folk have been known to swim between Donmouth and the harbour. In 1898 beach rescuer Henry Mitchell smeared himself with butter to keep out the cold and sustained by hard biscuits, bottled water and Bovril heated on a small oil stove in an escort boat set off from Abercrombie's jetty. A steamboat whistle signalled Henry was beyond the Broad Hill when a zephyr from the south drew him out to sea. With the swim abandoned Henry was cheered on his return to Fittie.

Above left: Bathing machines on Aberdeen Sands.

Above right: Aberdeen Beach.

B

Back Wynd

Back Wynd, or Westerkirkgate, is one of Aberdeen's oldest streets – 'Back' because it was then at the end of town, and gate (gait) which is Scots for road, later displaced by the Latin-derived *street* introduced from England. Today's Back Wynd is a truncated version of the road running from Schoolhill into Adie's Wynd and the Green down a slope.

The construction of Union Street cut across Back Wynd and eventually the slippery brae above the Green was replaced with a flight of narrow stairs, later widened and known more recently as the Boots steps from the time the store adjoined them.

Described as 'magnificent' during James VI's reign, the land populated with crofts and cottages around Back Wynd was granted a licence to feu so that much-needed houses might be built. One house, 'a sklayt-hous callit the Kirk Lodge', later became Aberdeen Song School. Since then more radical transformations have taken place with the old name retained.

John Barbour

Fourteenth-century Archdeacon of Aberdeen and poet John Barbour is renowned as the father of Scots literature. His epic *The Brus* recounts Scotland's Wars of Independence centring on the Battle of Bannockburn. This narrative of eyewitness accounts is among the earliest of native-penned works in Scots, besides Gaelic.

Archdeacon Barbour commemorated with a plaque near his Castlegate home.

Strongly nationalist, it is a romantic account of how Robert the Bruce and the Black Douglas stood firm against the tyranny of England's Edward I, Hammer of the Scots.

> A! fredome is a noble thing,
> Fredome mayss man to haiff liking,
> Fredome all solace to man giffis,
> He lyves at ess that frely lyvs.

Bestiary

Richly illustrated, the *Aberdeen Bestiary* is an encyclopaedia of the natural world as understood in the twelfth century and is regarded as the finest of medieval books of beasts. Being hand-written in Latin on parchment with lavish illustrations including birds, animals, plants and stones alongside biblical and morality tales suggests that it might have been a teaching tool. Produced in England, the *Bestiary* was part of the royal library at Westminster Palace until given to Marischal College by Thomas Reid.

Boece

Hector Boece (Boyce) was King's College's first principal. A philosopher and historian, he was a friend of the Renaissance humanist Erasmus of Rotterdam. Boece and Bishop Elphinstone established Aberdeen's first university, King's College, which they modelled on Continental universities. Boece lectured on divinity and medicine and created the Regius Chair of Moral Philosophy which continues today. An influential historian, his *Historia Gentis Scotorum* (*History of the Scottish People*) of 1527 was the second ever history of Scotland. Latin was the international language of learning

Aberdeen coat of arms.

and Boece's *Historia* translated into Scots became 'the oldest book of prose written in Scots to survive in modern times'. Boece's history flattered the Stuarts and was possibly behind the misrepresentation of Macbeth as a devious and calculating king now hard-wired into legend through Shakespeare's play of the same name.

Bon-Accord

French for good agreement, Bon-Accord hints at medieval Scotland's close ties with France and was the password at the storming of Aberdeen Castle in 1308 when an English garrison was routed during the Wars of Independence. Aberdeen paid a heavy penalty for its patriotism when in 1336 an English force reduced the city to ashes over six days of sustained terror and destruction when people and property were attacked and the town made bankrupt.

Bon-Accord became synonymous with Aberdeen and is incorporated into the city's coat of arms, street names, company and product names from granite to lemonade and what is regarded as the first fully illustrated comic, *Bon-Accord* of 1881. Important visitors to Aberdeen were received with a cup of Bon-Accord – 'Bordeaux wine, sweetmeats and spiceries' – and on departure toasted with 'Happy to meet, sorry to part, happy to meet again – Bon Accord.'

Bow Brig

Spanning the Denburn Valley at the edge of the old burgh, the brig provided access to the Green from the south between 1747 and 1851 and was where VIPs received a cup of Bon-Accord.

A bow meant arch, as in this bridge, and also referred to the city's ports or gates, collectively known as the 'bows' of the town.

Architect-mason John Jeans' replaced the 1550s twin-arched bridge with this single-span Bow Brig to better cope with the Denburn in spate. Country women hawked their knitted woollen stockings and fir-roots kindlers here on Fridays, engaging in the crack with townsfolk by the *loupin' on stane* stood on by older people to mount their horses more easily.

When the much-loved Bow Brig was removed to make way for the northern railway line a portion was incorporated into the arches of Union Terrace Gardens, although it is not apparent.

> The toon cooncillors came, when the loons were frae hame,
> Tore doon the auld brig (oh! Mair to their shame);
> Had the loons been there, faith, 'the man wi' the wig'
> Durstnae touched but a stane o the auld Bow Brig.
>
> (Davie Duncan)

City burns were crossed by lots of rudimentary bridges, including several Chinese-style brick ones over the Denburn – all of them now gone.

Breviary

Aberdeen Breviary was the first book printed in Scotland, a printing press having been set up in Edinburgh for that purpose around 1510. The two volumes of the *Breviary* – pars hiemalis (winter) and pars aestivalis (summer) – were reprinted at the behest of James IV as an assertion of Scotland's identity and nationhood. It includes accounts of Scottish saints such as Machar of Aberdeen and Moluag of Ross compiled by Bishop Elphinstone and Hector Boece. The book contains the first known calendar to recognise 6 July as the festival of St Palladius of the Mearns as well as the *Compassio Beate Marie* – a guide to religious services. Aberdeen University owns one of four extant copies.

Brig o' Balgownie

The elegant Gothic arched old Brig o' Don built by masons under Richard Cementarius *c.* 1320 is one of Scotland's few remaining ancient bridges. Who paid for it is unclear – perhaps the Royal Exchequer (it was promoted by Robert the Bruce) or the Bishopric of Aberdeen, as punishment for Bishop Cheyne's support for puppet ruler John Balliol. It remained the main crossing over the Don at Aberdeen before 1831 when a larger bridge downriver was erected.

Children love leaning over bridges and dropping items into the water. One such child was George Gordon, later Lord Byron, who many a time leaned over the Brig o' Balgownie despite being haunted by Thomas the Rhymer's verse:

> Brig o' Balgownie, Black's your wa',
> Wi' a wife's ae son, and a mear's ae foal,
> Down ye shall fa'!

Young George suspected himself to be the 'ae son' (only son) doomed to tumble into the waters below – the Black Neuk. Years later Byron included a reference in *Don Juan* to the Balgownie prophecy that scared him as boy:

The Brig o' Balgownie.

The Bridge of Dee.

As 'Auld Lang Syne' brings Scotland, one and all,
Scotch plaids, Scotch snoods, the blue hills, and clear streams,
The Dee, the Don, Balgounie's brig's black wall,
All my boy feelings, all my gentler dreams

Brig o' Dee

Built in 1527 of granite and sandstone, this seven-arched bridge improved access to Aberdeen on the medieval drover's road from the south despite the activities of determined stone thieves. Here on 18 June 1639 some 9,000 Covenanters under the Marquis of Montrose clashed with Charles I's army. The Battle o' the Brig o' Dee, the first encounter in the Wars of Three Kingdoms, was a victory for the Covenanters.

Even in peaceful times the bridge was guarded to prevent unwanted strangers from entering Aberdeen, such as those harbouring disease. A watchman's hut on the southern end was manned by day with no access at night. Great importance was placed on the watchman's role and anyone failing in his duty was fined, secured in the branks or had his 'lug nailed to the Trone' (burgh weighing machine).

Bruce

Robert I – Robert the Bruce, Earl of Carrack, the Bruce – was a late convert to the Scottish Wars of Independence; he famously switched sides, possibly scenting an opportunity for himself. Following Wallace's execution Bruce stepped up to lead Scotland's resistance against English aggression. He was crowned King of Scots in 1306.

The Bruce family's strong links with Aberdeen led to the king bestowing royal lands, notably the forest of Stocket, for hunting, timber cropping, cultivation, operating mills and fishing to the city in a charter dated 10 December 1319 (still held in city archives).

Butter

Aberdeen was once as famous for butter as Cheddar is for cheese. Twin Spires Creamery off Great Northern Road and named after St Machar's Cathedral's spires was a major producer, initially run by Aberdeen Milk and District Marketing Board.

Above left: Sculptor Alan Beattie Herriot's statue of Robert the Bruce outside Marischal College.

Above right: Bronze statue of George Gordon, Lord Byron, by sculptor Pittendreigh MacGillivray stands at the later Grammar School on Skene Street.

Curiously Aberdeen butter prompted a duel when an Englishman dining in a Glasgow coffee house complained the butter was unsatisfactory and demanded some of better quality. The waiter's insistence that there was none finer than Aberdeen butter elicited a furious rant disparaging all Scottish butter. Overhearing this exchange, the Laird of Culrossie piped up: 'That's nae true; Aberdeen butter is as good butter as ever gaed down your thrapple.' Anger boiled over and Culrossie was challenged to and fought a duel with small-swords in which he was wounded. He thanked his adversary for sparing his life but insisted, 'I'll say yet, that better butter than Aberdeen butter ne'er gaed doon a Southron's thrapple.'

Lord Byron

'Half a Scot by birth, and bred a whole one.'

Byron's mother was a Gordon of Gight near Banff and a descendent of Robert the Bruce. Byron's father was a dissolute sponger who squandered his wife's family fortune then abandoned her and their son, so the boy, known in Aberdeen as George Gordon, and his mama lived for a time at No. 10 Queen Street before moving around the corner to No. 64 Broadgate (Broad Street). From Longacre school George Gordon attended the Grammar School where he famously scored his name into a wooden desk. The small boy, dressed in bright yellow breeks who walked with a limp and had a reputation as a prankster, never forgot his Aberdeen childhood. In Venice in 1819 he and a fellow Aberdonian reminisced about the city with Byron speaking fondly of the Wallace nook and its statuette of a soldier and his dog.

C

Carden Place

Carden Place was named after Jerome Cardan, an extraordinary sixteenth-century Italian physician, astrologer and mathematician. Because of the interest he took in the town's water supply while visiting Aberdeen a Denburn well was named in his honour. In 1708 this well became the source of the town's first structured water supply – 'the first font (cistern) at the spring of Cardanus Well' and a variation of his name became Carden Place. Or so the story goes.

Castlegate (Castler)

Aberdeen's traditional market square measured 100 walking paces wide by 200 paces in length to enable two regiments of foot to stand in rank and file.

Here merchants granted trading privileges could sell their goods at weekly markets sanctioned by Alexander II and in 1273 an annual fair was authorized by Alexander III.

Little interrupted markets other than public executions, when the square was cleared so crowds could watch some unfortunate soul swing. The position of the gallows outside the Tolbooth is marked by a rectangle of granite setts.

From her lodgings in the Castlegate in 1562 Mary, Queen of Scots witnessed the beheading by the maiden (guillotine) of Sir John Gordon of Deskford. Three hundred years

The Castlegate.

Castlegate panorama.

later, in 1856, John Booth of Oldmeldrum became the last person publicly executed in Aberdeen. The city hangman was encouraged to stay in his unpleasant job with incentives such as the pick of fish and peats from Castlegate traders.

Some of Aberdeen's oldest buildings are in the Castlegate; town houses belonging to local rural gentry. Here, too, Aberdeen's first printing press, the Townes Armes, was set up by Edward Raban in 1622. Mixing the military with civilians could lead to tensions. In 1802 celebrations for the king's birthday ended in tragedy. Officers belonging to the Ross and Cromarty Rangers of the Highland Regiment stationed in Aberdeen antagonised locals who reacted with 'squibs and missiles'. The regiment fired into the crowd killing four and seriously injuring others before magistrates intervened to end the bloodshed. The atmosphere was highly charged and the Rangers quickly pulled out of town. Charges brought against officers for 'wilfull murder' ended in a legal stitch-up intensifying local bitterness. In an early example of crowd-funding a private prosecution of five soldiers resulted in two officers being found not guilty, two sergeants found not proven while a third officer fled and was outlawed. Bereaved parents were forced to travel to distant Edinburgh for the trial and were left with high legal costs.

Ceres

The Roman goddess of plenty gazes across the Castlegate from atop Archibald Simpson's 1842 North of Scotland Bank at the junction of Union and King streets. The delightful colourful terracotta figure of Ceres was designed by local artist James Giles and modelled by Nelson Routledge Lucas. Symbolising Aberdeenshire's rich produce, Ceres clasps a cornucopia of fruits and vegetables and is flanked by a moustachioed British lion.

Ceres.

Mitchell's Hospital, Old Aberdeen.

The Chanonry

Here canons of St Machar's Cathedral lived in magnificent properties later acquired by Aberdeen University. Attractive A-Listed H-shaped Mitchell's Hospital, founded in 1801 by Aberdonian David Mitchell, provided for widows and unmarried daughters of Old Aberdeen's merchants. In their blue uniforms the women spun and knitted, helping contribute towards their keep.

Common Good Fund

The Common Good Fund has been a valuable source of revenue for Aberdeen. Set up in 1319, the fund accrued income from lands given by Robert the Bruce in return for an annual payment of £213 6s 8d. However, its management by city Baillies has attracted criticism; seventeenth-century historian Spalding wrote of 'Magistrates wasting the Common Good in feasting and wine drinking'. What remained after council excesses contributed to the likes of Marischal College's expansion, the Art Gallery, Robert Gordon's College, Central Library, Fish Market, the road around Girdleness and purchase of lands at Ferryhill, Foresterhill, Hazlehead, Hilton, Kincorth and Rosemount.

Correction Wynd

The name shortened from Correction House Wynd came from a mid-seventeenth-century House of Correction founded under royal patent to confine 'vagabonds and minor delinquents'. Detainees were put to work making 'broadcloth, kerseys, seys

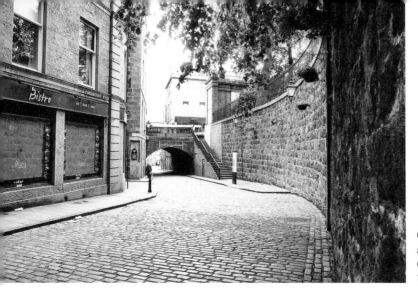

Correction Wynd, arch access to the Green and steps onto Union Street.

and other coarse cloths' to improve their morals – hence the name. The institution was costly to establish, 2,000 merks, and set up as a joint stock company to address the consequences of poverty and starvation at the root of inmates' problems. Hunger drove the desperate to riot, so-called meal mobs, in frustration over food hoarding by grain merchants. Unfortunately for the House of Correction the worst culprits were troops of various regiments garrisoned in the town who plundered so much stock the company sold up in 1711.

Here stood the *Breadhous* or town's hospital, a house and garden founded in 1459 by canon John Clatt to maintain burgesses and members of guild and demolished in the seventeenth century. The Wynd provided access to and from the Green and when Union Street was built overhead Correction Wynd and the Green were linked through an arch. A granite stair connecting the Wynd with Union Street was built in 1807.

Crooked Lane

Crooked Lane links Loch Street with St Andrew's Street in a crooked fashion. Once a hive of nineteenth-century industry, public baths and swimming pond, it is now reduced to being a mere handy, if crooked, lane.

Alexander Cruden

In 1737 Cruden compiled *A Complete Concordance of the Holy Scriptures*, an index of the Bible and the first work of its kind. Following studies at King's College Aberdonian Cruden became a bookseller and corrector of press (proofreader) in London. Unfortunately, Cruden was tormented by poor mental health, which might explain his carrying a small sponge each time he went out to wipe away pro-Jacobite graffiti during the 1745 Jacobite rising.

D

Dee

Aberdeen's southern river, the Dee, rises in the Cairngorm mountains, flows through Aberdeenshire and finally enters the North Sea at Aberdeen harbour.

The meandering Dee Estuary created little islands – Inches in Gaelic – a magnet for local children attracted by its pools: Doggie Lion, Pintler and Tide Pot to catch eels and bandstickles (sticklebacks); an eel skin wrapped around an ankle was a lucky charm for boys going into mock battles. In summer its pools were for swimming and in winter, skating, and at the 'toon's middens' trapping little sparrows was easy sport.

Reclamation of the Inches quickened pace in the nineteenth century when under an Act of 1868 the Harbour Commissioners diverted the Dee south of the Inches replacing bogs with solid ground made up of dumped rubbish, generating areas for industry – timber yards and sawmills, shipbuilding and fish kilns – but at the expense of drifts of mauve sea daisies (thrift).

The Dee Estuary and Inches.

Don

Aberdeen's other river is the Don. Smaller than the Dee, the Don springs from the Ladder Hills before dropping to the North Sea at Donmouth. Its position north of the city gave it an industrial role outside of Aberdeen but its global fame is largely thanks to Byron's poem 'Don Juan' (see Brig o' Balgownie).

Doric

The dialect of Aberdeenshire and Angus has a bond with Ancient Greece. The term Doric referred to Dorians, a much-disparaged community in north-west Classical Greece and so Doric became associated with a lack of refinement and applied to the lowest order of Greek columns.

The first pastoral poems were written in Doric (Greek not Aberdeen) by Theocritus in the third century BC. More Doric literature followed, which demonstrates the folly of snobbery over dialect. In the eighteenth century Scottish makar, Allan Ramsay, defended literature written in Scots or Doric (regarded as the same) with reference to Theocritus but it is a battle which endures.

Scottish Doric has distinguished itself in literature; William Alexander's *Johnny Gibb of Gushetneuk* is a fine example along with the poetry of Charles Murray, Marion Angus, Violet Jacob, Sheena Blackhall and, of course, Nan Shepherd. They have all reflected the people and landscape of north-east Scotland through their language in prose, poetry and song. One of Scotland's best-loved novels is Lewis Grassic Gibbon's masterpiece *A Scots Quair*, which is set in the Mearns, south of Aberdeen, although Gibbon tempered its Doric to broaden the book's appeal.

Written Doric is fairly easily understood with a little effort, for it is mainly phonetic. However, the dialect has its own rich vocabulary which can be challenging, e.g. qweets are ankles, kneeve a fist. Doric words are disappearing fast with lost generations and redundant occupations but the dialect survives sufficiently to bamboozle visitors to Aberdeen with such classic phrases as – fit like, min? foo y'daen? foos yer doos? (variations on how are you?) To which the standard reply is, aye peckin' (doing fine). If confused while shopping for shoes you might ask, fit fit fits fit fit? (which foot fits which foot?) or when asking if there's a bar nearby the reply might be, nane-I-ken-o (none I know of).

Duthie Park

Sitting alongside the River Dee at Great Southern Road, Duthie Park was created from land gifted by Elizabeth Crombie Duthie of Ruthrieston, to honour her brother and uncles. Designed by Dundonian William McKelvie, the park's 44 acres of shrubberies, trees, ponds, tennis courts, sculptures and grass for the young to 'frolic and play' opened in 1883.

Elizabeth Crombie's face looks out as Hygeia, Greek goddess of health, sculpted by talented granite mason Arthur Taylor. Several former redundant street fountains were moved into Duthie Park as decorative features along with a magnificent red polished Peterhead granite fountain of three basins and swans made for the park.

Figure of Hygeia in Duthie Park.

William Elphinstone

Appointed Bishop of Aberdeen in 1483, Elphinstone's name has since been synonymous with the city. An influential figure outwith the north-east, this lawyer and priest was a member of James III's council – foreign ambassador, auditor of the exchequer, chancellor and a senior appeal judge. He was also an envoy and Keeper of the Privy Seal for James IV and from their friendship Aberdeen got its first university by duplicity, it appears, with both men painting an exaggerated picture of an 'uncivilised' north-east corner of Scotland desperately in need of education and religious instruction to ensure papal approval in 1495. Elphinstone was keen that Scotland's would outnumber England's universities – not so hard since England had only two.

Despite Elphinstone's close relationship with James IV he failed to dissuade him from siding with France in its war against England, which resulted in his death along

Impressive bronze tomb monument to Bishop Elphinstone by sculptor Harry Wilson sits outside King's College Chapel.

with 10,000 fellow Scots at the Battle of Flodden on 9 September 1513. The infant James V was placed under Elphinstone's guardianship but a year later Elphinstone was dead, aged eighty-three.

Elphinstone was interred within the chapel but his remains disappeared during the Reformation. His name lives on through the university's Elphinstone Institute for the study of Ethnology, Folklore and Ethnomusicology.

The Enlightenment

The Scottish Enlightenment was a movement of ideas encompassing politics, science and philosophy that proved hugely significant and influential in the later eighteenth and early nineteenth centuries. Scotland as a major contributor to the movement surely reflects her regard for education. From the Reformation every Scottish parish could boast a school which fed into Scotland's five universities with their well-established links to Europe's great universities and scholars.

No dry intellectual movement, the Scottish Enlightenment generated spirited intercourse among individuals and groups with a penchant for good company and social drinking. Both gown and town intellectuals met regularly as Aberdeen Philosophical Society (the Wise Club) in taverns in Old and new Aberdeen.

Aberdeen's leading Enlightenment figures are discussed below.

James Beattie, Laurencekirk-born Professor of Moral Philosophy at Marischal College, was a vociferous opponent of Britain's slave trade long before its abolition in 1833: 'that a man, a rational and immortal being, should be treated on the same footing with a beast, or a piece of wood, and bought and sold, and entirely subjected to the will of another man, whose equal he is by nature ...' A poet and author as well as philosopher, Beattie famously challenged David Hume's atheism in *An Essay on the Nature and Immutability of Truth* in 1770. His poem *The Minstrel* attracted much praise, a royal pension and an honorary degree from Oxford University. Beattie urged his fellow intellectuals to suppress 'Scotticisms' and phrases and adopt English as the route to success in life. He was made a member of the American Philosophical Society in 1784.

Beattie's house in Crown Court, off the Upperkirkgate, became Aberdeen General Dispensary, Lying-in and Vaccine Institution and in more recent times the building was demolished for the Bon-Accord shopping centre which promised a consumer's paradise, squash courts, bowling hall and bar and delivered a fraction of this. What Beattie would have made of it is anyone's guess. He died in 1803 and was buried in St Nicholas graveyard.

John Gregory, Physician and Professor of Philosophy at King's, wrote *A Comparative View of the State and Faculties of Man with those of the Animal World* (1765) and *A Father's Legacy to his Daughters* (1761) in which he advised women to resist demonstrating their learning lest they scared off potential husbands, ideas rightly attacked by Mary Wollstonecraft in *A Vindication of the Rights of Woman*.

Beattie family gravestone in
St Nicholas graveyard.

James Dunbar, Professor of Moral Philosophy and later Regent at King's, is best known for *Essays on the History of Mankind in Rude and Cultivated Ages* (1780).

Thomas Reid, from Strachan (pronounced Straan) in Aberdeenshire was a graduate of Marischal College. He founded the Scottish philosophical school of common sense and his *An Inquiry into the Human Mind on Principles of Common Sense* (1764) became a seminal work of the Enlightenment and influential in the founding of the American republic.

For a time, church minister at Kincardine O'Neil, Reid returned to academia and became regent and professor at King's College before moving to Glasgow University. In 1783 he was involved in founding the Royal Society of Edinburgh.

George Turnbull was a theologian, philosopher and innovative professor at Marischal College who incorporated empiricism into his teaching of mathematics, science, history and politics by introducing students to botanic gardens, museums, laboratories and observatories. As well as innovative learning, Turnbull broke new ground with his works on moral philosophy and was a major influence on his pupil, Thomas Reid. Turnbull died in 1748 at The Hague.

George Campbell, a graduate of Marischal College, philosopher and Professor of Divinity wrote *The Philosophy of Rhetoric* and *Dissertation in Miracles*, which was yet another attack from Aberdeen on David Hume's atheism. His translation of the Bible from Greek was a labour of love. Campbell died in 1796 and is buried in St Nicholas graveyard.

David Skene, naturalist and philosopher, was born in Aberdeen in 1731. He attended the Grammar School and Marischal College before studying medicine and botany in Edinburgh, London and Paris. Later he graduated MD from King's College and as a medical doctor managed Aberdeen Infirmary. Skene became a Dean of Faculty at Marischal and collaborated with Linnaeus in the field of natural history, providing him with botanic specimens.

F

Fishing

Aberdeen's reputation for high-quality fish is long-standing. In 1290 a ship sailing from Yarmouth to bring the Maid o' Norway to Scotland to become queen was supplied with barrels of Aberdeen fish. That the little princess died en route to Scotland has never been attributed to anything she ate onboard.

In 1341 fishermen from Scotland and the Low Countries combined to protect each other's fishing boats against piracy. Aberdeen's links with that region were firmly established from early medieval times and perhaps it is not surprising that Aberdeen's merchants and magistrates purchased and fitted-out a fishing vessel in Rotterdam and engaged a Dutch skipper to fish for herring. How well the arrangement worked I have no idea, but herring did become an important source of income for the city as it was a species suited to preservation and to export. In later centuries barrels of pickled herring were regularly shipped out from Scotland to slave estates in the West Indies and with the decline of this miserable human trade from the 1830s herring exports struggled, more so with the loss of the Irish market following that country's famine and mass migration.

For over a thousand years Aberdeen was a thriving fishing port and exporter of fish. Records from the 1100s show the importance of salmon with vast quantities caught in

Trawlerman in
the 1970s.

the Dee Estuary and also from the Don. During the sixteenth and seventeenth centuries Aberdeen salmon fishers worked every day of the week netting vast amounts of fish; somewhere in the region of 360 barrels each weighing 250 lbs were exported annually to the Continent alone. Such rapacious scooping-up of fish stocks was condemned by kirk ministers as fishermen's greed. Back then fish lived long enough to mature and some huge specimens were caught. Those same kirk men would not believe the tiny fish taken from our rivers and seas today.

When fish stocks were strong prices were low, so fish was the perfect food to feed to servants. Transport costs increased their value. It was claimed a salmon bought in Aberdeen in 1653 for sixpence fetched 100 crowns in London. An exaggeration, surely, but Dee and Don fishers – and Aberdeen as a result – raked in fortunes off the backs of fish.

Sea fishing for white fish encouraged boatbuilding. Sail gave way to steam and steam to diesel. Aberdeen's first steam trawler was a converted paddle tug called *Toiler* launched in 1882. In 1887 white fish alone earned the port £87,000 (*c.* £10 million) rocketing twenty years later to £890,000 (*c.* £103 million.) In 1900 around 250 vessels, including drifters and line boats, sailed out of Aberdeen making it the largest white fish port in Britain. In addition, there was herring fishing and, for a time, whaling.

A range of subsidiary industries were born out of fishing, besides shipbuilding: net and barrel-making, engineering, ice and salt for packing and preserving, curing, and coal for steam engines. Market Street fish market was extended along Commercial Quay and Torry became the centre of fish processing.

Aberdeen fish market.

St Fittick's Kirk

Tucked into the hillside between Balnagask and the Bay of Nigg, the seventeenth-century chapel was abandoned and its congregation moved to Nigg Church in 1829. Churches had occupied St Fittick's site since early Christian times and in the twelfth century King William the Lion endowed the Abbey of Aberbrothoc (Arbroath) with monies to erect a chapel in what was described as a 'little glen full of quiet charm'.

Nothing so ancient survives at St Fittick's, although a fragment of its graveyard wall may be thirteenth century. As for St Fittick, he was St Fiacre, a seventh-century Irish saint with a talent for curing the sick, which will remind those familiar with St Fittick's church of its small window installed perhaps so lepers might follow church services without infecting the congregation with this dreadful disease.

One who lies buried at St Fittick's is Covenanter William Milne of Kincorth, killed on 10 July 1645 'for the cause of Christ, here rests in peace from his labours. This man, who piety, probity, and God's holy covenant made happy, fell by the sword of a savage Irishman.'

Before the Anatomy Act of 1832 availability of bodies for dissection was restricted, so medical professors and their students acquired corpses by stealth. Graveyard watch-houses provided shelter for families guarding the recently deceased from resurrectionists. Nevertheless, in 1809 Janet Young's grave was dug up and her body removed by a medical student who hid it at the Bay of Nigg until the coast was clear, but he fled abroad in fear of his own life. On another occasion a professor from Marischal was seen entering the college in a gig with a lady passenger who turned out to be a stolen body.

Links of a chain attached to the church wall might be a remnant of punishment: jougs, an iron collar placed around the sinner's neck and often attached to kirk walls. I suppose they might have been chains for cups to slake the thirst of churchgoers, but that might be wishful thinking.

St Fittick's
Church and leper
window.

Flittin'

Moving house traditionally took place on 'flitting day' – Whitsun Friday at the end of May or early June. The term 'flitting' comes from Old Norse *flytja*, meaning move, and when few people owned their own homes or stayed in accommodation attached to a job flitting was frequent, often annual. Wheelbarrows, carts and horse-drawn lorries were loaded up with dressers, bedding, pots and pans and on flitting day streets were noisy and bustling with so many people and their possessions on the move at the same time.

From 1883 tenement tenants in Aberdeen forsook the Whitsun Friday move for flitting on the stroke of midnight on a Saturday when the darkened streets would be packed with tired and excited families traipsing through the early hours of Sunday morning. City scavengers in the 1880s were given bonuses to be on hand to sweep up mess left behind from these mass flits following an order from a Cleansing Department inspector that no offensive matter such as chaff and soot should be left abandoned on the roads at such times.

Foresterhill

The people's hospital was opened in 1936 as Foresterhill Hospital, the result of money generously donated by the people of Aberdeen and its environs – hence its name. This was when governments did not generally pay for hospitals through taxation, so responsibility fell to communities. Hoping to raise £400,000 between 1925 and 1929, the campaign grabbed the public's imagination and reflected the need for improved hospital facilities, so money poured in. *The Silver Book* published by the *Bon-Accord and Northern Pictorial* contributed to the fund which finally raised £535,000.

The plan was to bring several hospitals together on one site at Foresterhill. A new children's hospital was first to open there, in 1929, transferred from Castle Terrace and it was joined by the maternity hospital (Matty) alongside the infirmary on former Silverhillock and Balegreen farmland.

Footdee (Fittie or Futty)

This popular bijou area of Aberdeen contrasts significantly with its humble beginnings as a fishing settlement on the city's sea edge and foot of the Dee. Fittie folk were fishers and St Clement, protector of mariners, their patron saint. A chapel dedicated to him was built *c.* 1498, its priest and upkeep supported through a local annual levy.

St Clement's Chapel deteriorated over time but in 1631 was reinstated by George Davidsone of Pettens, and a burial ground added. Unwanted attention during the Reformation and the wear and tear of centuries led to a replacement kirk in 1828. John

Smith's St Clement's East Church has long since shut its doors but its graveyard is packed with interest, if rather neglected. This inscription to Davidsone can be found on a wall:

George Davidsone, Elder Burges of Abd.,
Bigit this Dyk on his ovin Expenses,
1650.

Fittie's transformation began in the early nineteenth century when architect and superintendent of public works John Smith created two squares of house: north and

Right: A Fittie street.

Below: View towards Fittie from Greyhope Road.

south and known as Fish Town. These homes were owned and rented by the council, early public housing schemes; although pre-empting Margaret Thatcher they were soon after sold off to tenants.

Once famed for its fisherfolk and drinking houses per head of population, Fish Town and the larger community of Fittie went into a decline but emerged smaller and still a community. What is left of old Fittie – its gardens and tarry sheds – attracts new occupiers whose only connection with the sea is the driftwood outside their dainty houses. The gardens, mostly well-tended, remain but gone forever are Fittie's giant whale bone arches.

Freedom Lands

The name given to property purchased in the 1300s by Aberdeen burgesses to generate income for the city: Bogfairley, Countesswells, Cruives, Forresterhill (*sic*), Hazlehead, Northfield, Rubislaw, Sheddocksley, Tulloch, Kepplehills, Southfield and Westfield augmented lands provided by Robert the Bruce.

A series of boundary or march stones demarcated the Freedom Lands. Naturally occurring landmark boulders, earthfast stones, were used along with others brought

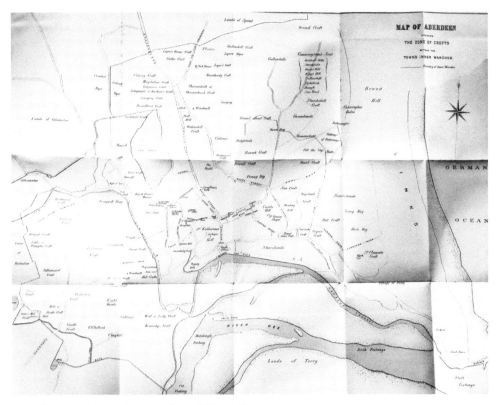

Map showing the Freedom Lands and March Stones.

March Stone at Jack's Brae.

in for the purpose. Inner march stones bore the initials CR for City Royalty or Regality and in 1790 the sixty-seven outer march stones which defined the 42 kilometres (26 miles) of Freedom Lands were inscribed ABD for Aberdeen out of concern that individuals were claiming property on the town's estate. Riding or walking the city's marches was once a popular activity.

Froghall (Frogha')

Froghall on the east of the city may have got its cute name from a haugh (hollow) full of frogs. It was certainly a boggy spot and long after attracting its name was still associated with animals through piggeries and cattle grazing. Less charmingly accumulations of animal dung augmented with human waste from the city surely created its own distinctive aroma.

Where there's muck there's much else besides and so it proved at Frogha' where among several productive gardens one run by a member of the Cocker family, later prodigious rose growers, cultivated fruit and vegetables for sale.

As Aberdeen's population grew housing and businesses swallowed up Froghall, ousting little Froghall Cottage and its acres of flowers and fruit. In came industries including the Jute Works, which left its echo in the name Jute Street, and Charles McDonald's granite works so that by the late 1930s little that was rural remained at Froghall.

Gallowgate

The Gallowgate was the old port entry into the city from the north and Old Aberdeen. In 1602 city magistrates ordered that a windmill be erected on Aberdeen's highest hill, Heidon's Hill, at the Gallowgate, paid for from local taxes. Industries powered by water from the old loch included rope, twine, linen thread, tanners and leather works. Here, too, was a Quaker meeting house and burial ground; a Poor's hospital for orphan and destitute boys; Gilbert Gerard's House for poor girls; and St Paul's Church where George Gordon, later Lord Byron, and his mother worshipped. The much-loved Co-op arcade occupied part of the Gallowgate from the 1920s until its misguided demolition.

The last battle fought inside the city took place in 1646 during the Wars of the Three Kingdoms when Royalist troops broke through the Gallowgate and in a bloody struggle crushed Covenanting forces at the Broadgate. The fifteenth-century Mar's Castle survived that skirmish but was demolished in 1879 when the Gallowgate was widened.

David Gill

Gill and outstanding photographer George Washington Wilson succeeded in taking remarkable photographs of the moon in 1869. Gill went on to combine photography with astronomy and in another magical moment he captured an image of the Great Comet streaking across the sky at Cape Town in 1882.

Apart from pioneering astrophotography Gill is remembered for his astronomical calculations. Prior to running the Cape Town Observatory, he helped establish a world-class observatory at Dunecht. During an illustrious career Gill received international recognition from global scientific bodies. He became president of the Royal Astronomical Society in 1909.

Born at No. 48 Skene Terrace in 1843, David Gill studied under the mathematical physicist James Clerk Maxwell at Marischal College, then briefly worked at his father's clockmaking firm before turning to astronomy. He died in 1914 and was buried in St Machar's graveyard. Sir David Gill has craters on the moon and Mars named after him.

David Gill's home on Skene Terrace.

Girdleness

A large rock shaped like a girdle (griddle) may have provided a name for this headland on the south side of the harbour. A lighthouse has stood at Girdleness since 1833. It was designed by Robert Stevenson, grandfather of the author Robert Louis Stevenson, to improve safety for vessels entering the harbour. Until 1870 when paraffin was introduced its light beam was fairly dull, fuelled by whale or vegetable oils. Eventually the lighthouse became automatic and is now controlled from Edinburgh.

Gordon's

At his death in 1731 Aberdeen merchant Robert Gordon left part of his fortune made trading in Danzig to found a hospital for the sons and grandsons of impoverished burgesses and needy sons of craftsmen from the Seven Incorporated Trades. At the end of the nineteenth century Gordon's became a fee-paying secondary school specialising in technical education. Gordon's Hospital became Robert Gordon's College and now Aberdeen has a Robert Gordon University.

Confusingly, the Gordon statue outside Gordon's College has no connection with the school but is of Charles Gordon of Khartoum. London-born of a north-east family, Gordon was a professional soldier and government bureaucrat whose involvement in

Gordon of Khartoum.

the Opium Wars earned him the nickname Chinese Gordon, but it was in Sudan he died in 1885 hacked to pieces, decapitated, his head displayed on a spear. Having fought for the British Empire and been the British government's dependable man overseas, Gordon was ultimately abandoned by it at the Siege of Khartoum.

Grammar School

Aberdeen Grammar School has been around since at least 1262, although not on the same plot. Originally it stood on Schoolhill, naturally, on the site of a Dominican friary, Black Friars, who gave their name to nearby Blackfriars Street. A later school of 1758 lasted until 1863 when the Grammar moved into a granite indulgence of Scottish Baronialism on Skene Street West.

Boys attending the Grammar had a reputation less for their commitment to academia than as unsavoury nuisances – theft, violence, vandalism, threatening behaviour with swords, firing guns and the like. The schools most prominent scholar and prankster was George Gordon, Lord Byron. Two teachers who probably struggled to contain the exuberances of their pupils were 'Crow Cromar and Jamie Watt, Chuckle head and girdle hat.' Don't feel too sorry for those masters and mistresses; they were not averse to flogging a boy held over the back of a school porter for convenience of the teacher.

Aberdeen Grammar School.

Granite

Granite is synonymous with Aberdeen, the Granite City. However, until the nineteenth century freestone was widely used for building. With granite came Aberdeen's distinctive and unique appearance aided by architects John Smith and Archibald Simpson.

Quarried stone brought wealth to Aberdeen, which for long dominated the granite trades. London's streets were paved with it, many of Europe's finest buildings were constructed from it and the docks at Sevastopol had their northeast granite docks blown up during the Crimean War under orders of Gordon of Khartoum. Aberdeen's highly skilled and innovative craftsmen became much sought after as masons and quarriers overseas. The most famous granite quarry in the city, Rubislaw, which became the largest man-made hole in Europe, stopped production in 1970.

The Green

In the Green rich and poor lived cheek by jowl in this former route into the town from the south. William the Lion kept a palace here. Robert the Bruce was an occasional visitor. His sister, Christian Bruce, was a resident. On the other side of the street, so to speak, was Lady Low, a woman with a reputation. Repeatedly banished for

The Green.

prostitution, she habitually returned despite threats of branding or being drowned in a sack. She was eventually branded on both cheeks while wearing a paper crown and banished for seven years and a day.

When Union Street was built above the Green and before it was lined with buildings pranksters found it amusing to chuck stones down the chimneys of homes in the Green to the consternation of residents. On the other hand, attic dwellers in the Green were able to clamber out windows and walk along planks stretched onto Union Street, effective if peculiar shortcuts.

In the Green many tragic events unfolded – massacres and destruction at the hands of English troops during the Wars of Independence and Protestant fanatics during the Reformation when a friar was hurled back into his burning Carmelite monastery. Here stood the notorious barn where kidnapped children were held prisoner before being sold.

Increasingly the Green became the focus of trade and commerce including the annual Pasch Market selling Scottish linens.

Guestrow (Guestra')

The Guestrow survives in a truncated form, just. It was called Goblin Street 500 years ago because of its proximity to the Mither Kirk's graveyard – or that spooky variation on Guestra, 'ghaistra'. Some suggest Guestrow referred to the boarding houses found there. In the 1930s the arch into Shepherd's Court was preserved and transferred to Provost Skene's House when Aberdeen's love affair with the demolition ball removed most of this street.

H

Harbour

For around a thousand years Aberdeen harbour has been central to commerce in the town. Established under David I in 1136, it is the oldest business in the UK. Over time merchants with deep pockets to fill pushed for the development of bulwarks and quays so larger mercantile vessels could dock safely. This mammoth task involved diverting the Dee and removing the muckle rock known as Knock Maitland or Metellan which threatened to scupper improvements. David (Davie-do-a-thing) Anderson succeeded where others had failed in shifting the obstruction when in 1610 he secured air-filled wooden casks to the giant boulder which floated away at high tide.

Quays were built and the North Pier extended to alleviate difficulties caused by the sandbar at the harbour mouth and the South Breakwater was erected to shelter vessels from easterly winds.

The council-run weigh-house checked imports and exports. Pre-Union weights and measures varied across Scotland with each town setting its own. A pound of meal, salt, honey and iron in Aberdeen was equal to 17 oz and 15/16 drachms, i.e. above the standard Scottish weight, and an Aberdeen pint was a quarter greater than the Scottish standard pint.

Tourism prospered during the nineteenth century. Visitors disembarking from steam packets were met by black-suited porters (shore porters) in 'Scotch caps' who hoisted trunks and bags onto a frame secured on their backs before loading them into waiting omnibuses. To southerners Aberdeen had all the appearance of a foreign city

Aberdeen harbour offices, Trinity Quay.

with its broad 'unintelligible' dialect; its 'French style porters'; and women with long earrings and 'tall white caps, muslin neckerchiefs and coarse aprons'.

More recently the harbour has sustained the offshore oil and gas industries and before that fishing and shipbuilding. The harbour is still a ferry port linking mainland Scotland with Orkney and Shetland.

The Hardgate

The Hardgate translates as a roadway set with stones; a causeway. Prior to Union Street's appearance it was the main western route to and from town, the Old King's Highway. Industries congregated around the Hardgate including a tannery, woollen works making tweed and the Aberdeen Wincey (linen/cotton mix), distilleries and breweries. Not surprisingly given its antiquity and location at the edge of town, the Hardgate witnessed several bloody encounters, most famously in the 1644 Battle of Justice Mills fought between Royalists and Covenanters.

Cocky Hunter

Cocky Hunter's is one of those names embedded into the very being of Aberdeen. Cocky Hunter sold *a' thing*.

> If ye want a knocker fer yer door
> Or a hoose tae fit yer floor
> Ging tae Cocky Hunter's stored
> In Aiberdeen.

You could be fairly confident of finding whatever you were searching for in Cocky Hunter's if you didn't mind raking through the shambles inside and outside Hunter's stores including Hunter's Emporium and Depository at the former sick kids' hospital on Castle Terrace. The Emporium was either a buying opportunity or eyesore with beds, bikes, lamps, wardrobes and plain junk spilling out over pavements and clambering up walls.

Thomas (Cocky) Hunter
(1867–1925) memorial in Trinity Cemetery.

I

Incorporated Trades

There were considered to be three classes of people in early medieval Aberdeen: merchant burgesses, craftsmen and common people. Most powerful were merchant burgesses or Guildry (except for an elite of 'gentlemen' considered born to govern), so to protect their interests craftsmen of the seven most esteemed trades formed an Incorporated Trades body. These seven trades were in order of importance: Hammermen, Bakers, Wrights and Coopers, Tailors, Shoemakers, Weavers, and Butchers. Only a Burgess of Guild or member of a trade association was permitted to open a shop or sell his own products as a way of controlling the quality of goods produced.

The Trinity Hall (Taranty Ha') is the meeting place of Aberdeen's Seven Incorporated Trades. Their present headquarters on Holburn Street is their third home. The first was at the Shiprow at Putachieside in a former Trinity Friars monastery gifted to them by Dr William Guild 'To ye glorie of God and comfort of the Poore, this Hows was given to the crafts by Mr William Guild, Doctor of Divinite, Minister of Abdn: 1633'.

The original Trinity Ha' gateway and second Trades' Hall on Union Street.

Here the trades met for around 200 years until in 1847 they transferred to Union Street, into an impressive building with Tudor-arched windows and decorative pinnacles. At its rear in the Green the original Ha's magnificent stone gateway was installed but broken up in the 1890s.

In 1967 the Trades moved into the present Taranty Ha', something of a monstrosity on the outside despite a series of splendid stained-glass windows depicting the arms of the seven trades. Inside, however, is a treasure house of apprentice pieces, craft models and paintings including an unusual portrait of William the Lion.

Indian

Before the twentieth century any Indian reference in Aberdeen was usually in connection with a sculpted head or a disgraceful period in the city's history.

Let's take the head first. Canada House on Union Street and home to the Headquarters of the North of Scotland Canadian Mortgage Company added a head of a Canadian Indian (Canadian First Nations) above its doorway carved from red granite. It is a fine head designed by sculptor Pittendreigh Macgillivray, but who the mason was I don't know.

Indian Peter was Peter Williamson who sued Aberdeen's baillies for slander after they charged him with libel. He won and received £300 damages plus legal costs, a tidy sum in 1758, from Aberdeen's provost, baillies and a Dean of Guild whose defence attorney was Walter Scott, father of the novelist.

Peter was kidnapped aged eight when child trafficking was rife in Aberdeen between 1740 and 1746. Thousands of children stolen off the streets fed this lucrative

Carved head above the doorway at Canada House.

trade. They were confined – including at 'the barn' in the Green, the Tolbooth and a manufactory at the beach – before being put onto Atlantic-bound vessels and sold as indentured servants to plantation owners. The price of a child was £16.

Unlike African slaves, indentured servants were freed after a number of years of servitude and sometimes provided with land of their own. Peter was bought in Philadelphia by fellow Aberdonian Hugh Wilson, also a victim of child trafficking, who bequeathed him his possessions. It's a long story but back in Scotland and something of a showman in full 'Red Indian' dress Williamson was nicknamed Indian Peter. His autobiography was confiscated in Aberdeen, torn up and burnt at the Mercat Cross by the hangman. Peter was charged with libel, found guilty, fined five shillings and banished as a vagrant. He turned up in Edinburgh where his life took a turn for the better. It was there he died aged sixty-four in 1799.

Infirmary

Aberdeen's first infirmary opened at Woolman Hill in 1742 to accommodate twenty patients. It became a royal infirmary in 1773 on receipt of its first royal charter.

Woolmanhill was one of several city hospitals: the Vaccine Institution of 1803 provided free inoculation at the Poor's Hospital, the City Hospital for contagious diseases was built out of the way at the Links in 1872, Maternity and Children's hospitals, Belleville hospital for Incurables at the Denburn along with convalescence homes and a Dispensary of free medicines. Asylums, places of safety and more in keeping with the old understanding of hospital, were provided for those mentally ill, blind, deaf,

Simpson's pavilion at the former Royal Infirmary, Woolmanhill.

orphans and the destitute. Woolmanhill's limitations for expansion prompted the Joint Hospitals Scheme and transfer to Foresterhill's 150-acre site in the 1930s.

Ironside

The name is unfamiliar today but John Ironside and Company, Wine, Spirit and Ale Merchants, General Bottlers of Ales and Stout to the Trade and Mineral and Aerated Water Manufacturers of Rosemount Viaduct, was very successful in its day. Purity was the term associated with Ironside's products. The factory's lead water pipes were lined with silver tin to prevent contamination and the water in its mineral and aerated beverages was filtered through charcoal to remove contaminants. Ironside's filtered everything: their own and bought-in wines and spirits for bottling – clarets, Champagnes, ports, beers, stouts soft drinks. The company claimed their stockrooms held every known blend and vintage spirit in addition to their own whiskies: Balgownie and Glentana (recommended for invalids).

Ironside's produced the unique Granite City-conditioned beers and stouts. This was the first company in Aberdeen to replace push-out stoppers with screw tops to retain freshness in opened bottles of beer and soft drinks.

Ironside's vast array of effervescent drinks came in response to a fad for all things fizzy following an article in *The Lancet* that claimed everything bubbly, from soda water to Champagne, promoted good health. Ironside's health drinks included kidney strengthening Lithia water and Potass to aid digestion.

John Ironside died aged sixty-two years in 1914.

DENBURN VALLEY ENTRANCE.

DUTY PAID WAREHOUSES, & MINERAL W
FACTORY.

John Ironside and his premises at the Viaduct and Jack's Brae.

J

George Jamesone (1586–1644)

George Jamesone is Scotland's first recorded portrait painter – and what a painter. Having studied under Rubens in Antwerp along with Van Dyck, it is hardly surprising Jamesone's style assimilated Dutch with Scottish influences. Jamesone was the leading portraitist in the British Isles and limner to Charles I.

Jamesone was a nephew of Davie-do-a'thing Anderson who shifted the muckle stane at the harbour. His father was a builder and the Jamesone home-cum-studio was a wonderful castellated house on Schoolhill, opposite St Nicholas Kirk and known as the Old Manse. Among its interesting features were walls decorated by Jamesone, a ship's oak beam incorporated into a turret, an immense oak door hung on huge

George Jamesone's house, Schoolhill.

iron hinges, a fireplace decorated with 'beautiful little Dutch bricks' and cavity-wall insulation provided by hops.

There was an outcry when Jamesone's, house which had been sold to carters Wordies, and used as a common lodging house, was demolished to widen Schoolhill instead of being preserved as Rubens' house in Antwerp had been.

Jamesone provided funds to repair the Well of Spa next to the Four-Neukit Garden where he kept a second home also 'paynted all over with his owne hand'. This property, too, was pulled down. Mary, daughter of Jamesone and his wife, Isobel Tosh, stitched magnificent tapestries which hang in the West Kirk of St Nicholas.

George Jamesone kept a house and studio in Edinburgh, the capital being a rich source of portrait commissions. He died there and was buried in Greyfriars cemetery.

Joint Station (Jynt Station)

Aberdeen Railway Company's Ferryhill terminus was not exactly handy for town passengers on the southern line, so in 1854 it was replaced by Guild Street station. The northern line's terminus was at Waterloo near the harbour and before that at Kittybrewster. With the Joint Station rail lines serving the north, south and Deeside all came together in one place from 1867.

The station was rebuilt between 1913 and 1920 and has undergone subsequent alterations.

Justice Mill

Justice Mill, first recorded in the 1300s as a water-powered mill in the vicinity of present-day Union Glen, is most associated with the Battle of Justice Mill of 13 September 1644 which claimed the lives of many townsfolk. An ominous blood-red moon shone over Aberdeen on the eve of battle between Charles I's evangelising army and Covenanters. Aberdeen's magistrates supported the Covenant, so local men were ordered out to defend the cause in the 'Fecht o' Aberdeen'. Approximately 4,000 royalists and 900 horse overwhelmed the Covenanters and wreaked slaughter, rape and devastation in the town over three days.

'the enemie entring the toune immediatelie, did kill all, old and young, whome they fand on streittes.'

Those murdered were stripped and dumped and anyone attempting to retrieve a body or openly grieving was instantly killed. Anger and resentment felt by townsfolk was great and long-lasting but peace returned and the blood-soaked cornfields where the battle took place around the How Burn at the Hardgate would in time provide oats for meal and barley malt for the city's brewers.

K

Kelly's Cats

Aberdeen's little black leopards line up along the north parapet of Union Bridge. Leopards or sometimes lions have adorned versions of the city's changing coat of arms. Those charming leopards perched on the bridge were added following its widening in 1905. Leopards decorated the south side too, but during the destructive 1960s when the south parapet was removed for some very dodgy architecture in the shape of shops those cats had to be rehomed – in the Central Library and Duthie Park.

Kelly's cats may have had nothing at all to do with William Kelly the architect whose name they adopted for some believe they were designed by Sidney Boyes of Gray's School of Art.

Kelly's cats at Duthie Park.

Kirkgate

The Upper- and Nether- (Lower) kirkgates provided access to the Mither Kirk before nineteenth-century St Nicholas Street interrupted the run of the Netherkirkgate between Correction Wynd and Broad Street. In the 1960s Marks & Spencer were given permission to extend their store, virtually obliterating the Netherkirkgate including removal of the historic Wallace Tower from the city centre.

The Upperkirkgate fared a little better. One of the city's few old streets, it hints at its former glory on one side only; shield your eyes from the other. The building with the lovely feature of sundials is seventeenth century; the one with its gable end on to the street was built when pends and closes intersected this part of town and entry was from the side; No. 6 is a melange of recycled architectural styles from as early as the sixteenth century complete with a gateway modelled on the Scots College in Paris.

One or two recollections of its inhabitants long dead filter down through time, such as a woman who kept her hand in the pocket of her pea-jacket and wore a man's hat on her head. The hat was said to have belonged to her betrothed who died in his youth and by wearing his hat she kept him close to her. What she kept in her pocket is not known.

One of two sundials at No. 24–26 Upperkirkgate.

A glimpse of Upperkirkgate.

Kitson

Kitson lamps shone a light not only on Union Street between Union Bridge and Holburn Street but on man's obstinacy. These incandescent oil lamps were popular across the Continent, America and with Aberdonians during their trial but a few councillors insisted on their removal irrespective of their low operating costs (half that of electricity). The press sided with locals and railed at Provost Fleming, describing him as 'after the manner of men suffering from obstinacy and rigidity preconceived opinion, which even facts plain and probed will not upset...' for claiming he would have the Kitson lamps removed even if their replacements cost eight times their running costs. Despite a well-subscribed petition to save the lamps, the 'plump for electricity at any cost' councillors keen to promote Aberdeen's new electricity plant won the argument.

Kittybrewster

> *Her yaird had midden-cocks and game,*
> *And mony a cacklin' rooster;*
> *She was a canty, kindly dame,*
> *They ca'd her Kitty Brewster.*

Cadenhead's rhyme plays to the legend of a tavern keeper called Kitty Brewster who was so admired the area took her name even if she ran 'a modest stob-thackit hostelry for men and horses'. As usual the truth is less romantic for Kittybrewster probably was a *cuitan briste* – broken cattle-fold in Gaelic and cattle mart. It became an unlikely transport hub with a toll bar and weighing machine controlling charges on the Inverurie Road where, incidentally, the toll keeper watched a falling star on its noisy descent into Ashgrove on the evening of 10 September 1850. The canal between Kittybrewster and Port Elphinstone offered passengers transportation on a fly boat until railway mania sunk the canal company and for a time Kittybrewster station operated on the Great North of Scotland Railway.

Library

Scotland was well supplied with libraries before the Library Act of 1867 but not all were free. Providing a municipal free service taxed Aberdeen Town Council, but in 1884 it edged closer in that direction by taking over the large library run by the Mechanics' Institute.

It was on 5 July 1892 the majestic Central Library opened on Rosemount Viaduct to much razzmatazz not generally associated with libraries. Aberdeen Artillery Volunteers' band made a tuneful racket and Aberdonians crowded round to watch Scottish-American tycoon Andrew Carnegie, a contributor to the library fund, open it to the public. In almost no time community branches sprang up, with dedicated reading rooms, library vans and a children's library.

Aberdeen Central Library and St Mark's Church before HMT was built.

Links

The Queen's Links have a justifiable claim as home to the very first golf course. Early sixteenth-century references to *goiff* and *goiff ballis* appear in the city's historic registers. However, at the time Aberdeen Town Council viewed this newfangled pastime as dangerous, an 'unlawful amusement', and proscribed it in 1565. Golf fanatics were certainly playing it in 1625 at the Queen's Links and in 1642 John Dickson was permitted to make *gowff ballis* in the city. In 1780 Aberdeen's Society of Golfers was formed.

That other sport of gentlemen, horse racing, took to the 'two mylls of lenthe' of the Links whose 400 acres were very often out of bounds because of military drilling, so much so the council petitioned parliament to stop them in 1871 to have sewage works installed. In any case they were a nuisance for townsfolk using this common land for sports and drying fishing nets. As for those sewage workers they could not imagine the horror that lay ahead when bodies of some of the 2,000 plague victims forcibly isolated at the Links in 1647 were exposed during their excavations.

Lion

The lion lounging on his pedestal within the curved recess at the Cowdray Hall is surely the pride of the city. Designed by Aberdeen sculptor William MacMillan, the lion was carved by James Philip assisted by George Cooper from Arthur Taylor's granite works in Jute Street.

For thousands of years lions, the king of beasts, represented courage and faithfulness – hence their popularity with monarchs to symbolise power, e.g. Scotland's twelfth-century William I or Lion. The lion came to represent the British Empire and troops fighting in its wars. It is in this role that Aberdeen's lion guards the Hall of Remembrance. The loss of 10,000 Gordon Highlanders (mainly from the north-east) during the First World War led to calls for a cenotaph in Aberdeen. However, Kemnay's pale granite 'as white as the undriven snow' was criticised as unbefitting at the lion's unveiling in 1925.

The Lion.

Loch

Look at any ancient map of Aberdeen and one of the first things to strike you is the loch close to what is now the town centre – think Loch Street. It was not the only watery area of Aberdeen but certainly its biggest.

The boggy ground surrounding the loch, called Lochlands, was fed by burns trickling through pastures rented out, *roupit,* for animal grazing. Birds used the loch and Parson Gordon described the loch as 'white wi' Geese and grey wi' Gu's' (gulls).

The loch attracted industry: waterwheels powered mills (Flourmill Brae) and lysters (dyers) among the businesses who both depended on it and added to its pollution; human waste contributed to making it hazardous for drinking but its water was sold from barrels by *burne beirers (*water-sellers) as washing water.

The filthy state of the loch encouraged the council to provide fresh drinking water through street fountains. Fresh water sellers, licensed for 10 merks annually in the seventeenth and eighteenth centuries, were in demand. Lizzy was one. Scrupulously clean she filled her pails to the brim but was targeted by mischievous boys who would bump against her spilling her water. Whenever this happened Lizzy emptied what remained in her pails, returned to the well and patiently waited humming while rocking to and fro, moving her hands as though spinning. With her pails refilled she set off again to deliver to her customers.

Magistrates ordered the loch be drained in 1603 but little happened for two centuries.

Lodge Walk

A short residential street between Castle Street and Queen Street got its name from the Freemason Lodge housed within the New Inn. Next to the Tolbooth Aberdeen City Police were based here until 1979.

Remains of sixty-three executed men and women were unearthed when Lodge Walk's graveyard was disturbed during building work in 1892. These were people hanged since 1829. Before then those executed were disposed of through various means – dismembered and hung up in public until their skeletons fell apart; thrown into the sea or handed over to anatomists for dissection – so a shaded grassy spot in Lodge Walk was paradise by comparison.

The first woman buried there was the last woman hanged in Aberdeen. Catherine Humphreys murdered her husband in 1830. 'Lord God if anybody would give him poison and keep my hand clear of it' she had often pleaded before pouring poison into his open mouth as he slept. His screams, 'I'm burned – I'm gone – I'm roasted' alerted neighbours. 'Oh, woman, woman, you have tried to do this often, and you have done it now' he lamented. He died two days later in agony with his widow insisting his death was due to 'bad drink', but an empty phial of vitriol (sulphuric acid) and acid-burnt bedding told a different story. Humphreys later confessed and walked to the gallows with her eyes averted from the 12,000 spectators gathered on Castle Street to see her hang. Catherine signalled to the hangman she was ready to die by dropping her handkerchief then whispered, 'Oh, my God.'

Lodge Walk.

St Machar's Cathedral

St Machar's Cathedral provides an iconic image of Old Aberdeen. Legend has it sixth-century St Columba instructed his disciple St Machar to set up a church at a bishop's crosier-shaped bend in the River Don. He obeyed and a church has occupied this spot since then. In the twelfth century St Machar's became a cathedral, which has been rebuilt and altered over time.

St Machar's widespread diocese paid for its upkeep and canons' manses along the Chanonry. Inevitably the cathedral's huge estate proved a temptation for priests with worldly ambitions such as Bishop William Gordon who distributed diocese landholdings among his family.

The Protestant Reformation separated St Machar's from more of its property. Its roof lead and bells were removed for shipping to Holland but never got beyond Girdleness where the boat sank – perhaps a message there. Several manses were destroyed, estates sold and the cathedral's status reduced to a parish church. Cromwell's troops contributed to the vandalism by partly demolishing St Machar's for its stone to reinforce their stronghold on Castlehill.

St Machar's
Cathedral.

MacGillivray's warbler.

William MacGillivray

Renowned ornithologist William MacGillivray was born in Old Aberdeen on 25 January 1796. He spent his childhood both in Aberdeen and Harris and the 360 miles between he covered mainly by foot, which provided MacGillivray with ample opportunities to study nature. The lack of roads and transport led people to walk vast distances and MacGillivray also walked all the way to London to visit its museums.

Having studied medicine at King's College, MacGillivray was for a time curator at the Royal College of Surgeons of Edinburgh but returned to Aberdeen in 1841 to become Professor of Civil and Natural History at Marischal College. His five-volume *History of British Birds* became an essential text for ornithology students everywhere and a source for Charles Darwin's *Descent of Man*. MacGillivray's recognition of hooded and carrion crows as separate species took 150 years to confirm.

MacGillivray and American ornithologist John James Audubon were friends and collaborators with Audubon providing bird skins to Marischal zoology museum. The MacGillivray warbler species found in the Rockies was named after William MacGillivray.

The Mannie

The modest little lead figure intended originally to be golden and affectionately known as the Mannie stands atop the Castlegate well. This fountain erected around 1706 became Aberdeen's first public well, with open-mouthed green men's heads. The Mannie offered the discerning consumer spring or river water at the turn of a handle and enjoyed a sojourn in the Green but returned to his roots in Castle Street.

The Mannie as street art.

Marischal College

Alexander Marshall Mackenzie's dramatic 'granite wedding cake' neo-Gothic façade of Marischal College, the second largest granite building in the world behind el Escorial in Madrid, is now the headquarters of Aberdeen City Council. In a previous existence

Marischal College.

Marischal College was a university in its own right before being incorporated with King's to form the University of Aberdeen in 1860. Archibald Simpson's university buildings lie behind the façade, around the quadrangle.

Market Street and Markets

Archibald Simpson's hand is in plain view in the avenue of granite that is Market Street. How it must have glittered when first built – a new order imposed over medieval Aberdeen's twisting lanes of timber, tile and turf dwellings.

A market was built, naturally, on Market Street. The Market Hall opened with pomp before a crowd of 4,000 people on 29 April 1842. A vast shopping palace, its basement included seventy-four shops and 250 stalls, several fishmongers, while greengrocers and fifty-four *dead-meat* butchers occupied the main floor. On the higher level virtually anything and everything was available for purchase; the Market Hall was regarded as one of the best in the UK. Then it burned down on 29 April 1882 – forty years to the day after its opening.

Its replacement failed to capture the magnificence of the original but proved popular, so when the council decided to demolish it opposition was strong, to no avail. Down it came in 1972 and a mini version of no architectural merit was installed below a department store.

The Market Hall 'tidied up' and absorbed a plethora of street markets. No more need for the sounding of a horn and call – 'Too too, roo too, fine caller 'oo', Sellin' i' the Squaar jist i' the noo' – but competition for fishwives who for centuries traded at the old Fish Cross on Castle Street before being moved to the Shiprow in 1742 following complaints from businessmen of being splashed with mess from haddock, Colliston speldings, partins, lobsters, rawns, dulse, etc., as they walked across the Castlegate.

Market Street.

Huxter Row (huxter means trader), whose stallholders sold everything from spunks and besoms to butter and poultry (Turkey Willie with a turkey tucked under his oxter and singing the Jacobite song 'Come through the heather, around him gather ... for wha'll be king but Charlie; and his wife Betty were there each Friday'), was demolished in the 1860s.

At the turn of the nineteenth century Aberdeen's fifteen slaughterhouses supplied a huge numbers of fleshers (butchers) trading at the Mercat Cross (the High or Flesh Cross) and forty others on George Street. Markets were held daily at the Gallowgate and Chapel Street and weekly in the Green once Union Street replaced it as the town's principal thoroughfare. The Corn Exchange on Hadden Street off the Green kept going into the 1950s.

Aberdeen's bakers outnumbered even its fleshers. Sweet-toothed Aberdonians were invited to secure Jupiter's gingerbread by hitting it with a bawbee at his shore stall. Those with poor aim forfeited their penny and some disgruntled customers resorted to hurling Jupiter's cakes with stones or pieces of coal out of frustration.

Baker Jacob Blackwell's specialities were his mutton pies and 2-inch round lemon 'cakie topped with sweet confections'. As well as a stall at the Castlegate he sold directly from his Flour and Treacle Depot, the former Pitfoddels Lodgings (now law courts), with its large hearth fitted with 'snug berths' where children waited while Blackwell's pies baked. They would juggle them, piping hot from the oven, careful to prevent the hot rich gravy leaking out while servant lassies carried away fresh pies for their employer's dinner on plates covered with crisp white napkins.

The timmer market has never really left but is not what it once was – a market for all things wooden held on the last Wednesday in August selling everything from ladders and wash tubs to spurtles and fir root firelighters.

Aberdeen has had its share of memorable traders: Pie Bob at the Castlegate selling his ha'penny pies; Blin' Bob who was Duncan Mackinley and sold everything from shoelaces to the latest scandal broadsheets (a popular singer he died in poverty in 1889); Italians imploring folk to buy plaster figurines of Robert Burns, Souter Johnnie and Napoleon with their refrain 'will ye buy, will ye buy?'

In 1935 the Castle Street market moved a short distance to the market stance between Justice Street and East North Street. The Friday and Saturday 'castler' was

The New Market, restored.

both treasure trove and junkyard and produced its own characters such as Kempie and his much-put-upon sister Mabel and where Bronco Bill pulled teeth and entertained onlookers at one and the same time.

Francis Masson

This botanist from Old Aberdeen became Kew Gardens' first plant hunter. To satisfy British gardeners' cravings for rare and unusual plants Masson was dispatched to South Africa aboard Captain Cook's ship *HMS Resolution* in 1772 to hunt out the exotic. He sent back over 500 different specimens and immediately set out again on his quest. However, setting foot on unfamiliar territories was not risk-free. Imprisoned by the French in Granada he was also captured by pirates while crossing the Atlantic to New York. Masson died in Canada in 1805 and was interred in the Scotch Presbyterian Churchyard at Montreal.

McCombie's Court

A covered lane between Union Street and the Netherkirkgate, McCrombie Court was named after Councillor Thomas McCombie, tobacco and snuff manufacturer, and was Archibald Simpson's first completed commission (running alongside his house for the Laird of Auchintoul on Union Street) and the start of a lang sang for Simpson and Aberdeen.

McCombie's Court.

Hugh Mercer

Mercer studied medicine at Marischal College and joined Bonnie Prince Charlie's army as an assistant surgeon. On the run after Culloden and its bloody aftermath Mercer sailed to America where following a brief spell with the British Army defying American independence he switched sides. A brigadier with the revolutionary forces, Mercer and George Washington became close friends. At the Battle of Princeton in 1777 Mercer was bayoneted by his former redcoat comrades and died of his injuries, aged fifty-one.

Mercer's reputation is preserved in American place names and on a statue at Fredericksburg, Virginia, he is described as 'bravely defending the liberties of America'. There is a modest plaque commemorating him in Marischal College quadrangle. Old Blood and Guts, General George S. Patton was Hugh Mercer's great-great-great-grandson.

Monkey Brae

Sometimes known as Wellington Brae, this handy lane between Prospect Terrace and Wellington Road cuts beneath the railway line and has been at the forefront of several disputes over responsibility for its upkeep. The curious name is down to a real monkey kept by the owners of a booth called *the shop in the wa'* at the brae foot. The monkey earned its keep turning the handle of a barrel organ to attract customers – so much more interesting than Wellington Brae and more deserving.

Monkey Brae.

Monkey House

'I'll meet you at the Monkey House' has been repeated down the generations. Named because of its semicircular Doric colonnade – its monkey bars – it was built for the Northern Assurance Company and since has housed offices, restaurants and bars. Its liberally decorated exterior is repeated inside with fine intricate plaster detail.

Mounthooly, Mounthilly, Mounthoolie

Perhaps a holy hill, it was windy Mounthooly with its windmill and windy Mounthooly with its Split the Wind (Split the win') or Cleave the Wind at the north end of George Street and Powis Place where A. Marshall Mackenzie's church beautifully defines the chevron-shaped feature isolated Mounthooly, with its smallpox hospital and earlier still Lepers Croft run by monks shown on Parson Gordon's map at the end of what became Love Lane between the old and new towns of Aberdeen.

The name Mounthooly was meant to vanish in 1894 when the council planned to absorb King's Crescent, the Spital and College Bounds into the High Street. Fortunately, this never happened.

The Music Hall

Union Street's bold architectural statement from Archibald Simpson with its grey granite Ionic columns was originally the Assembly Rooms. The élite from both town and county fancied a select venue for balls, dinners, billiards and meetings, so following a successful appeal for funds the Assembly Rooms opened on a very 'coorse' day in April 1820. The torrential rain might have been an ill omen for the Assembly Rooms failed to make money and in 1858 it was sold to the Music Hall Company who created a concert hall that opened to the general public in 1859.

A 1950s postcard of Union Street with the Music Hall on the extreme left.

Once admitted the public enjoyed all kinds of activities beyond concerts. Roller skating took the 1930s by storm with skaters rolling from town to town and competing in endurance events held at the Music Hall. Aberdonians Robert Bruce and Hadyn Maxwell pulled in crowds to watch their skating marathons in which contestants ate, shaved (optional for women) and attended toilet needs while skating (again, more appropriate for men). On 14 January 1931 Aberdonian Fred Laverton beat Hebden Bridge's Arnold Binns' world record of sixty-one hours eighteen minutes. Reluctant to accept defeat, Binns declared he would not leave Scotland without the roller-skating record. But he did.

Mutton Brae

Mutton Brae in the Denburn Valley was a higgledy-piggledy collection of red-tiled dwellings accessed by steps from Schoolhill. In earlier times crofts dotted the area and in 1693 there were concerns the grass was being 'eaten up and destroyed by flocks of sheep', which might be the source of Mutton Brae's name. An alternative suggestion is that the Denburn's muddy flanks led to it being called 'mud toon'. Take your pick.

Mutton Brae shoemaker and leather-worker Beau Aiken habitually wore a Kilmarnock nightcap, two coats (one back-to-front), a leather apron and knee-breeches. His funeral in 1850 descended into farce when his daughter insisted his coffin was opened and she proceeded to take out 'a good feather pillow' from under his head, replacing it with wood shavings.

Mutton Brae.

N

Saint Nicholas

Aberdeen's Mither Kirk is dedicated to the city's patron saint, Saint Nicholas. Since 1430 he has appeared on the town seal and coat of arms and was once celebrated with a fifteen-day market each October from 1557.

St Nicholas Kirk was completed in 1498, the largest parish church in Scotland. It was divided into two churches at the Reformation, their congregations decided by street lot – the 'Grene and Crukit' quarters of town attended the Auld Kirk while 'Evin and Futty' inhabitants went to the new one. The oldest grave in St Nicholas dates from 1463; incorporated into the wall of Collison's Aisle, it contains the remains of Provost Alexander Chalmers.

Until the Reformation St Nicholas Church was prosperous, maintained by obligations and bequests. In the fifteenth century kirk-building expenses, including twenty merks yearly for mason's pay, were paid from kirk taxes: four groats were taken for every sack of wool and each 'cloth of skins' exported to Flanders and Zeland from Aberdeen while fishers contributed annual duties. In addition to actual money virtual currency in the form of fish and skins augmented its income – e.g. the revenue from 287 half barrels of salmon along with assorted fish and dozens of Futefel (sheep skins). Not every arrangement was consensual. Englishman Thomas Borrow resented having to accept four-and-a-half lasts of salmon for supplying St Nicholas with ten fodder of lead for its roof in 1507.

It is not clear the mischief played by Walter Strachan and fellow kirk singers that resulted in their dismissal in 1532. Paid twenty shillings annually plus their 'meat' (any food), they were fired 'for their demeritis bigane' – possibly making free with church property, 'sklayttis, tymmer, and stanis' (slates, timber and stones), for as fast as building materials entered the church they left under someone's simmet. Kirk authorities were strict. John Anderson was fined 6s 8d for lingering 'in the wedding door' while wearing a bonnet and in 1672 Dean of Guild Thomas Mercer was fined the astronomical sum of 500 pounds Scots and obliged to 'take his tongue in his hand, and say "False tongue he lied" ' for publicly insulting ministers of the town.

The graveyard, now popular for a quiet sandwich at lunchtime, was where young George Gordon sought refuge beneath a tombstone during a fierce snowstorm

St Nicholas Kirk from Back Wynd.

and where resurrectionists raided graves. Notorious anatomist and bodysnatcher Andrew Moir was exposed when a dog scraped up human remains at his premises in St Andrew's Street (then Hospital Row). Moir and his students ran for their lives pursued by furious Aberdonians. As he hid in the cemetery he knew well Moir's rooms were burned down and when he died aged thirty-eight he was buried, and remains so, in St Nicholas graveyard.

Bay of Nigg

Nigg is perhaps named after a Celtic chief, Cormac de Nugg, mentioned in a thirteenth-century charter, although Nigg is a common Scottish place name – *an Neag* in Gaelic means notch in a hill and appropriate here. William the Lion gifted fishing and farming at 'Nig' to the monks of Arbroath in the late 1100s.

The Bay of Nigg has been developed into a deepwater berth for cruise ships.

O

The Round O (Roon O)

The Roon O was a curiously named feature seen on older city maps. Scoured-out hollows from glaciations produced the Roon O at Ferryhill and the Kettle at Old Aberdeen. The Roon O lent itself to legend. One Sunday evening the minister and elders of a little kirk on the hollow were playing an illicit game of cards when at midnight there was a great flash of lightning and the Devil, *aul Hornie*, materialised dancing around the Roon O as the church and its guilty gamblers were drawn downward into Hell.

Soapy Ogston

The name says it all; a man called Ogston produced soap. For 200 years Ogston's manufactured soap and candles at the Gallowgate with Soapy joining his grandfather's company, producing award-winning soaps such as Balmoral and Elegance. Boiling fats and oils to make soap and candles was hazardous. On 15 April 1888 a huge blaze ripped through the Loch Street factory and another in 1905 resulted in substantial job losses.

More trouble came five years later when Ogston, then in partnership with Tennant, makers of Kilty Carbolic, were accused of selling underweight products by the *Daily Record*. Ogston & Tenant sued the newspaper and won. In view of this the *Daily Mail* having run the same story and its owner Lord Northcliffe quickly settled out of court.

Ogston & Tennant eventually amalgamated with Lever Brothers, which later materialised as Unilever.

Ogston & Tennant, Gallowgate.

The Piper Alpha memorial in Hazlehead Park.

Oil

Aberdeen mutated from Granite City to Oil City almost overnight on 6 March 1967 when North Sea natural gas was piped onshore. Forecasts of the industry's decline have been greatly exaggerated over the past fifty years. Offshore industries became major sources of employment and fostered high-skilled engineering jobs in and around the city. However, Aberdeen has little to show for its key role in this multi-billion-dollar international business. The oil city has seen no ambitious architectural features or civic amenities provided. There is a sculpture of offshore workers in the rose garden at Hazlehead Park commemorating the 167 victims of the Piper Alpha tragedy on 6 July 1988.

Old Aberdeen

Auld Aberdeen, Aulton, was until 1891 distinct from new Aberdeen and can claim Aberdeen's first university, King's College, the magnificent St Machar's Cathedral and the Tillydrone motte.

Above left: Seventeenth-century engraving of Auld Aberdeen.

Above right: Old Aberdeen trades coats of arms.

Old Aberdeen Town
House and Mercat Cross.

Auld Aberdeen was made a Burgh of Barony in 1489 by James IV, thus enabling it to erect a Mercat Cross around which weekly markets and two annual fairs were held – Skyre fair on the Thursday before Good Friday and St Luke's fair on 18 October. Local craftsmen were obliged under threat of fines to confine trading their goods to Old Aberdeen rather than selling at new Aberdeen's markets. Livestock was sold at the Glebe where horse trading continued until 1933. The following year Aberdeen Town Council ended Aulton's 400-year-old market, although there's been something of a token revival since.

Attacked during the Reformation but ultimately following actions of the council in the eighteenth century what remains of the Mercat Cross stands before Old Aberdeen's Town House. The 1788 Town House bears the burgh coat of arms and motto *concordia res parvae crescunt* – Little things grow through harmony.

Picturesque Wrights' and Coopers' Place, named after one of the Aulton's six incorporated trades along with Grant's Place and MacRobert Memorial Garden, presents an impression of how the old town once looked.

Oscar

Oscar was a whaling ship that foundered off Aberdeen on 1 April 1813 with just two survivors from a crew of forty-six. In gale-force winds *Oscar* moved out of the harbour seeking safety in deeper water, but as her anchors dragged in the strong flood tide she was driven onto the Bruntscallie rocks at Greyhope Bay. Onshore horrified spectators watched wave upon wave swamp *Oscar*. Her frantic crew chopped and sawed down masts to use as bridges to the shore but these were swept away. Gale-force winds battered *Oscar* until its timbers creaked and split apart. Desperate men slipped into the water but only two made it ashore – steersman James Venus and young John Jamson clinging to wreckage and retrieved by his uncle, a retired whaling skipper. Bodies recovered were taken to Sugarhouse Lane for identification then carted to St Fittick's Kirk where they lay head to head on pews until burial in a mass grave.

Palace Hotel

Scotland's dramatic scenery and history has proved a magnet for tourists and the wealthiest booked into one of Europe's finest hotels, Aberdeen's Palace Hotel in the heart of the city with direct access to the railway station including a private covered platform.

Opened in 1891, guests could ascend a grand white polished marble staircase to its 100 bedrooms, mostly en-suite, or take an American-manufactured lift. The Palace offered every sort of luxury: electric lighting; a host of public areas including reception, coffee, drawing and reading rooms all beautifully furnished; and a billiard room decorated with gold and leather.

The Palace's unique system of heating and ventilation involved 'air-washing' – water was filtered through coconut fibres to produce clean air at a steady 60 degrees. Exquisite food was provided by French chefs who pandered to the desires of royalty and film stars including Clark Gable.

The Palace was partly destroyed in a tragic fire in October 1941 in which six people died including two sisters and a sixteen-year-old girl employed as a housemaid two days earlier. It was demolished in 1950 and replaced by a utilitarian building housing various businesses including a C&A store and later Travelodge and bank.

The Palace Hotel's reception.

Patagonian Court.

Patagonian Court

Once washed by the tidal Denburn, Patagonian Court was a commercial storage, loading and unloading point for imports and exports such as guano for fertilizers shipped in from Patagonia. Small craft (lighters) ferried salmon, fleeces, hides, cloth, wool and porter to ships lying at anchor in the natural harbour of the Dee's mouth while salt, wine and pottery discharged from ships was stored in warehouses at Patagonian Court.

With Aberdeen's changing topography this busy thoroughfare between Back Wynd and the Corbie Haugh became a relic of a former age. In 1906 a programme of street improvements threatened the removal of Patagonian Court but, so far, it has survived, as a shortcut onto Denburn Road.

Peacock's Close

Formerly Skipper Scott's Close off the Castlegate, it was renamed after Francis Peacock (1723–1807), Aberdeen's official dancing master for sixty years. Dancing was regarded as an essential social skill and from 1695 Aberdeen employed a dancing master to instil 'manners and good breeding' in townsfolk. Peacock's first classes were held across the Castlegate in the Earl Marischal's lodging until its demolition in 1766 so Marischal Street might be built. Peacock went to Drum's Lane at the Meal Market and finally to Skipper Scott's Close. Soon Skipper Scott was usurped by Peacock. Peacock's bow being multi-strung with painting as one of his interests it is fitting that Peacock Printers set up art printing in Peacock's Close.

Pittodrie

Pittodrie became home to Aberdeen Football Club (the Dons) at its founding on 14 April 1903 following the amalgamation of Aberdeen, Victoria United

Alex Ferguson and fan celebrate Aberdeen FC's victory in the European Cup Winner's Cup in 1983.

and Orion. Pittodrie became Britain's first all-seater and all-covered football stadium and the first to install a dugout. The club colours are famously red and white, although before 1939 players wore black and gold vertical stripes and the terraces echo to cries of 'c'mon ye reds'. Aberdeen Football Club's domestic and European success includes European Cup Winners' Cup and the European Super Cup titles in 1983.

Provost Ross's House

Ross's House on the Shiprow is integrated into Aberdeen Maritime Museum. Marginally younger than Provost Skene's House, it was built in 1593 and home to city provost Ross between 1710 and 1712. Merchant Ross traded principally with Holland and died in Amsterdam in 1714. His house crumbled gracefully over time until restored in 1954. It is typical of Aberdeen architecture of the period with tower and decorative moulding around the doorway.

Provost Ross's House.

Gargoyle on Provost Skene's House.

Provost Skene's House

Much altered, Skene's was vandalized, threatened with demolition, subject to assault by concrete and commandeered during the second Jacobite uprising by Butcher Cumberland en route to Culloden. Provost George Skene once called it home and while not the first resident of this sixteenth-century town house, his name has stuck to it. In 1953 it was turned into a museum. A gargoyle on its exterior belonged to baker George Russell from nearby Ragg's Lane. When ordered to shut his bakery Russell blamed the move on a neighbour's complaints, so he had the man's likeness made into a gargoyle, which he attached to his house. In 1959 Ragg's Lane was demolished and the head transferred to Provost Skene's House.

Queen

The Queen's image that has dominated Aberdeen for centuries, staring out from the Mercat Cross, is that of Mary, Queen of Scots. Queen Street's persona was Charlotte, Electress of Hanover and wife of George III. A third queen, Victoria, is commemorated in streets, a bridge, park and two statues. The first was sculpted in 1866 in Sicilian marble by local artist Alexander Brodie. It stood at the junction of St Nicholas Street and Union Street and was regarded as very fine, but the ravages of weather drove this Victoria inside to shelter under the Town House staircase where she remains.

A hardier bronze by C. B. Birch in 1893 replaced Victoria at St Nicholas Street until 1964 when she flitted to Queen's Cross from where she gazes longingly towards Balmoral Castle.

Above left: Unveiling of Queen Victoria's statue, 1866.

Above right: Queen Victoria at Queen's Cross.

R

Tinny Robertson

Tinny was tin can manufacturer John Robertson. Born in 1864, John was apprenticed as a tinsmith and moved to London when an Aberdeen canning and preserve factory, Morton's, opened a branch there. Tinny was one of many workers from Aberdeen and Dundee who followed the factory south.

Anything that could be canned was – from fish to hair oil – and port cities like Aberdeen and London were at the heart of this trade provisioning the military, maritime trades, British Empire, local and export markets. Morton's London branch was based at Millwall dock and its workforce played football during breaks, including Tinny. Millwall Rovers football club is said to have been formed by tin workers with Tinny instrumental in its development. Tinny was bitten by the football bug and following his return to Aberdeen where he opened his own business in St Paul Street, and later Roslin Street, he joined the Board of Aberdeen Football Club, becoming its chairman in 1930 until his death in 1935.

Rowies

Rowies, butteries, rolls are all the same thing: flattish, doughy or flaky rolls with plenty of salt and fat. They are quintessentially an Aberdeen speciality, although widely copied. Gone are the heady days of Buttery Willie's heated trays to retain the aroma and freshness of his rolls hot from the oven and precious few, if any, contain butter. Grumbles began over 150 years ago when lard started to replace butter: 'it puts you in mind of the chemical works, bones and old shoes ... lard! lard!' complained local author and buttery aficionado William Buchanan.

For generations of Aberdonians a baker's paper bag with greasy spots blooming from the warm rolls inside promised nectar of the gods. Sadly, few craft bakers are left in Aberdeen and rowies come cold, in plastic bags from supermarkets.

Among celebrity appreciators of the rowie is film director Duncan Jones, son of David Bowie, who spent part of his childhood in the city with his Aberdeen nanny, Marion Skene. Duncan developed a liking for the delicacy and now makes his own butteries. From Zowie Bowie to Zowie Rowie.

Aberdeen rowies.

Rubislaw Quarry

Lying west of the city, Rubislaw Quarry provided the bulk of stone that went into creating the Granite City. Rubislaw provided gathered stone since the 1600s, but with the construction of Union Street and transformation of the city centre quarrying went deeper until Rubislaw ended up as the biggest man-made hole in Europe at some 450 feet. The council-owned quarry was sold to Skene of Rubislaw for £13 in 1788 – yet another misjudgement from the Council Chambers as Rubislaw proved to be a goldmine, in a sense, a granite mine, from which vast fortunes were made.

S

Setts

Often mistakenly called cobbles, setts are small rectangular-shaped granite stones also known as cassies and once used for paving roads (cassie is short for causeway – a made road). Millions of setts were produced in Aberdeen to line local streets but were also exported in vast quantities and a major source of local revenue.

Granite setts.

Nan Shepherd commemorated on a £5 note.

Nan Shepherd

Poet, author, book reviewer and hill walker, Anna (Nan) Shepherd, born on 11 February 1893 just outside Aberdeen, is best remembered for her lyrical descriptions of the Cairngorms. A niece of William Kelly, of Kelly's Cats fame, Nan graduated from Aberdeen University in 1915, becoming a lecturer at Aberdeen Teacher Training Centre until her retirement in 1956.

Nan's novels, *The Quarry Wood* published in 1928, *The Weatherhouse* and *A Pass in the Grampians*, capture the distinct nature of north-east life. *In the Cairngorms*, a collection of poetry, was published in 1934 while Nan's highly acclaimed work *Living Mountain: Celebration of the Cairngorm Mountains of Scotland*, written a decade later, went unpublished until 1977. In it she explores her great affinity with the hills – her 'Buddhist's pilgrimage to the mountain', the 'journey into Being'.

Nan Shepherd, along with friends and colleagues including Jessie Kesson, J. C. Milne and Charles Murray, promoted dialect literature in the face of snooty criticism. The literary establishment's disdain for the likes of Doric meant Shepherd's work was largely undervalued and her talent as a major author went largely unrecognised during her lifetime.

On a memorial stone to Nan Shepherd at the Makars' Court outside the Writers' Museum in Edinburgh are her words: 'It's a grand thing to get leave to live'. Nan Shepherd died at Woodend Hospital on 23 February 1981, aged eighty-eight years.

Shipbuilding

Boatbuilding in Aberdeen is as old as this maritime trading town. Not the first vessel but the first recorded Aberdeen-built ship was *Bonacord* (*sic*) made for Alexander Davidson, a timber merchant (tymmerman) from St Andrews, in 1609.

Through the nineteenth and into the twentieth century around 3,000 ships were launched from the city's yards: Duthie, Walter Hood, John Lewis, Hall, Russell, Alexander Hall.

Aberdeen ships included one of the fastest clipper ships on the high seas, *Thermopylae*, built by Walter Hood's yard for Aberdeen White Star Line. Designed for

The clipper *Thermopylae.*

speed, these mast and sail cargo vessels mainly shipped high-value items from the Far East such as tea, opium and spices. *Thermopylae* best demonstrated William Hall's Aberdeen bow (which first appeared in *Scottish Maid* out of Alexander Hall's yard in the 1830s) when *Thermopylae*, striking with green hull and white sails, cut her more famous rival *Cutty Sark* down to size, beating her in a record-breaking sixty-three days between Shanghai and London in 1872.

Until the opening of the Suez Canal Aberdeen clippers could compete with their steam rivals but eventually steam proved their nemesis. *Thermopylae* was transferred to the Australian wool trade and later ferried Canadian timber and rice before being sold to the Portuguese navy in 1897 as a training vessel and coal carrier. Thermopylae's final days were inglorious; the Portuguese used her for naval target practice and she was sunk off Portugal in 1907.

Shore Porters' Society

One of the oldest surviving co-operatives on record from 1498, Shore Porters, whose profits were distributed between members, may go back to the 1100s. These porters/pynours/pyners carried goods to and from commercial vessels and were distinct from backmen or street porters employed in the rest of the town. Poynernook Road has no direct link with poyners but marks a local occupation.

In 1666 horse and van services were added to the business and porters helped with firefighting by providing cartloads of barrelled water to tackle blazes.

Given the importance of trade with the Low Countries it is hardly surprising Aberdeen Council had a thumb in the early Shore Porters' pie, but by 1850 the society was independent. More recently Shore Porters took over an English removal company but their headquarters remains in Aberdeen.

Archibald Simpson

Simpson was something of a celebrity architect for he and John Smith shaped Aberdeen during its granite years. Born on 4 May 1790 at No. 15 Guestrow, Archibald

Bon-Accord Crescent.

attended the Grammar School, a fellow pupil of George Gordon, Lord Byron. When he finally plumped for a career in architecture Simpson not only studied classical design in Italy but became conversant with the practical strengths and weaknesses of timber and stone.

Simpson favoured classical styles, exemplified in the former Medico-Chirurgical building on King Street – Aberdeen's first public building by a local architect. This commission demonstrated the merits of granite as a building material that lent itself to crisp classical lines. Arguably Simpson's finest achievement was Bon-Accord Crescent commissioned by the Corporation of Tailors, nineteen two-storey matching houses beautifully proportioned behind a graceful palisade of iron railings that separated them by a road from private gardens which dropped down to the Howe Burn.

Mary Slessor

Mary was born in Aberdeen on 2 December 1848 either at her grandmother's house on Mutton Brae or her parent's home in Short Loanings. She and her devout mother worshipped at Belmont Street's United Presbyterian Church.

When Mary was eleven the family moved to Dundee for work in the jute mills but Mary's mind was on higher works and following missionary training she sailed in August 1876 to Calabar to live among the Okoyong people of South Nigeria who came to call her Ma. She challenged their traditional prejudices such as suspicion of twins and adopted several abandoned children who were taught to read, doubtless with an Aberdeen accent for it was said she never lost hers. A missionary for thirty-nine years, Mary died in post in 1915.

Polished granite memorial with bronze inset commemorating Mary Slessor's missionary work, Union Terrace Gardens.

John Smith's colonnade on Union Street.

John Smith

Smith was Aberdeen's first appointed city architect, in 1807, and contemporaneous with Simpson. Unlike Simpson he was born into the life – his father was mason-cum-architect William Sink'em Smith.

Smith and Simpson were afforded a unique opportunity to make their mark on the blank canvas of newly constructed Union Street. Most of Smith's city works were fairly classical but his country mansions were often designed with Gothic-Tudor flourishes, resulting in his nickname Tudor Johnny. Smith's granite colonnade separating Union Street from St Nicholas graveyard is, however, determinedly classical and functional.

Spital

Matthew Kynismundie, Bishop of Aberdeen, founded a hospital here during the reign of William the Lion and the name was shortened with usage. Hospitals were refuges for the indigent and infirm rather than the medical institutions they became. Here, too, stood a leper house to contain this dreadful disease and a burial ground for when the inevitable occurred, across the road from the Snow Church.

Tenements

In the late eighteenth and nineteenth centuries people flocked to Aberdeen for jobs. Many were accommodated in tenements – two- or three-room flats mostly, even for large families, with the poorest reduced to sublets in cramped lodgings.

Of variable quality, tenements were well-loved by generations of Aberdonians before council schemes provided roomier alternative accommodation in the 1950s and 1960s. Conversion grants in the 1960s led to bathrooms and hot water taps being incorporated into flats, within a bed recess or corner of a room, making redundant the shared lavatory on the stair landing or outside in the 'backie', which literally froze in cold winters.

The drudgery of laundry was carried out in the communal washhouse in the back garden. A coal fire heated water in the boiler and once washed bedding and clothes were squeezed through a mangle before being hung out on ropes to dry.

Theatres

Haliblude (Holy blood) played at Windmillhill in 1440. The passion play was the earliest recorded theatrical act in Scotland and brought to Aberdeen by local merchants trading with the Low Countries where religious theatre was popular.

From the grassy *playe greens* of Windmillhill and Woolmanhill on the outskirts of town spectators enjoyed all sorts of entertainment brought by travelling players. The Abbot and Prior of Bon-Accord (the Abbot and Prior of Unreason) were elected annually to ride

Aberdeen tenements,
Esslemont Avenue.

the streets enticing people to join them in wreaking havoc and fun – cross-dressing and masks were encouraged for games, comic dramas and dancing on holidays.

Lots of stone and mortar theatres followed, including at Marischal Street (later converted into a church in a twist on current practice); Shoe Lane, later a stable; and Coachy's Playhouse on Chronicle Lane, where it cost half a crown for the pit and one shilling and sixpence for gallery benches where the 'eccentric schoolmaster known as 'Mad Sinclair' directed audiences.

The Tivoli Theatre on Guild Street began life in 1872 as Her Majesty's Theatre and Opera House, rebranding as the Tivoli in 1910. Compact and handsome, it joined the bingo craze of the 1960s but is again a theatre.

His Majesty's Theatre (HMT) of 1906 winked at the Italian renaissance in its design by theatre architect Frank Matcham with its tower, copper dome and pediment. HMT is 'damnation' in the attractive line of granite buildings along Rosemount Viaduct – Education, Salvation and Damnation (Aberdeen Central Library, St Mark's Church and His Majesty's Theatre).

Tillydrone

The name Tillydrone is a corruption of the Gaelic Tulach Droighne (knoll with thorn trees). Tillydrone's motte mystifies archaeologists. Suggestions are it might have been a Bronze Age burial cairn, second-century defences or base for a twelfth-century castle. The seventeenth-century Wallace Tower has a settled provenance. It was relocated here from the city centre against the wishes of Aberdonians in the 1960s.

Tolbooth

The Mids o' Mar (Middle of Mar), the north-east equivalent of Edinburgh's Tolbooth the Heart o' Midlothian, had twin functions: as a prison (High Tolbooth) and

The Tolbooth and Mercat Cross.

Town Chamber (Laigh Tolbooth). It also inadvertently fulfilled another role as a shipping aid when steersmen aligned the spires of the Tolbooth and St Nicholas Kirk to navigate a safe course into harbour.

For a time entry to the Tolbooth was by the first floor up a double flight of steps. There in 1817 two youths, their hands tied to the stairhead railing and backsides exposed before a curious crowd, each received fifty lashes from the city hangman for stealing. One of the last public floggings in the town, it failed to achieve its aim as the pair, Rossie and Buckie Haddocks, continued thieving and were later banished for fourteen years. However, that day an emboldened Rossie was overheard saying, 'Never min', Buckie, we're nae gaenn tae be hang't yet.' If they had been the Tolbooth's brand-new clock would have been silenced while the sentence was carried out.

Torry

The village across the River Dee from Aberdeen was only incorporated into the city in 1891. William the Lion presented the bulging hill or tòrr (Gaelic) to the Abbey of Arbroath and 300 years later it became a royal burgh when in 1495 James IV granted the fishing communities of Upper and Nether Torry a Charter of Barony. This provided its tradesmen and fishers with enhanced privileges including consent for weekly markets and a four-day annual fair to celebrate its patron saint, St Fotin (Fittick).

With the German Ocean to the east and the Dee to the north, it was inevitable many in Torry depended on what water could provide and not so long ago salmon fishers' boats were strung along the banks of the Dee. Line fishermen ventured into deeper water out at sea for their catches. Experienced boatmen, Torry folk were often pilots navigating safe entry to and from the harbour while others were employed as lumpers loading and unloading cargos.

For long Torry comprised two streets, Foreclose and Back Close, plus a school. The construction of Victoria Road was a signal Torry had outgrown its wee village status and Torry Farm controversially acquired by the City of Aberdeen Land Association (CALA) led to the development of new roads: Grampian, Oscar, Glenbervie, Menzies and Walker. Torry's population burgeoned from under 3,000 in 1891 to 14,000 by 1906, dropping to around 9,500 today.

Victoria Road, Torry.

Salmon fishers' boats and
Victoria Bridge.

Until 1830 when the Wellington Suspension Bridge (Chain Briggie) was constructed,
Torry was linked to Aberdeen by a small ferry. Not until 1881 was Victoria Bridge
erected to ease pedestrian and wheeled traffic and that came about as a consequence
of the tragic ferry disaster in 1876.

Torry Battery

Overlooking Aberdeen harbour, Torry Battery contributed to the country's coastal
defences. Built in 1860 and staffed by volunteers, it was decommissioned in the 1890s but
brought back into use during both world wars. In the 1930s and again after the Second
World War the battery was used as homeless accommodation with the last families
moving out in 1953. Scheduled as an ancient monument and despite its decrepit state, it
is a favourite location for watching dolphins and seals swimming at the harbour mouth.

Town House

Formerly known as the County and Municipal Buildings and dating from around 1870,
this handsome civic headquarters was given a Flemish flourish with a hint of Gothic
by architects Peddie and Kinnear – a nod to Aberdeen's ancient trade with the Low
Countries. Built from Kemnay granite, it is a symphony of architectural grace, with

The County and Municipal
Buildings, 1868.

ribbon columns, arches, tower and pepper-box turrets. A sundial on its south wall carries the motto 'UT UMBRA SIC FUGIT VITA' (Life flies like a shadow), a sentiment unlikely to find agreement from those detained by the law courts on the ground floor.

Tunnels

A network of tunnels dissects Aberdeen, some ancient and others less so. It is possible there were escape tunnels running through Castlehill and smugglers' tunnels between the town and sea. Storage tunnels dug underground by town businesses and long since abandoned have been found incorporated into buildings. Mostly bricked off, they await exploration. The construction of Union Street over a series of arches created subterranean streets in the likes of Carnegie Brae and the arch entrance from Correction Wynd to the Green while others simply disappeared. Tunnels were dug to carry electricity cabling, Post Office telephone lines, gas pipes and sewage. In the 1860s extensive sewerage excavations involved huge iron pipes snaking underground beginning under shoemaker John Airth's house on Market Street. Brick and concrete sewers, some 6 feet high, run the length and breadth of the city, but no longer is raw sewage discharged into the sea at Point Law and Girdleness but processed in sewage works at Balnagask.

Ventilators installed for the safety of workers are most visible on Hutcheon Street and Justice Mill Lane where a beautiful art nouveau-style shaft *c.* 1905 was installed to cool the intense heat generated by underground electricity cabling.

Above left: Tunnels at Carnegie Brae.

Above right: Ventilator at Justice Mill Lane.

U

Unicorn

A pretty little white marble unicorn with gilded spiral horn sits in splendid isolation atop the Mercat Cross. Bound with a golden chain, it holds a shield with the royal arms of Scotland. A unicorn has graced the Mercat Cross for over 400 years, although this one and its Corinthian column are modern replacements; the originals are preserved in the Tolbooth.

Unicorn, the mythical untameable beast representing purity and grace, was adopted as a symbol of Scotland's sovereignty and independence and often featured on Mercat crosses. Paired unicorns have appeared in Scotland's royal coat of arms since the reign of William I, the Lion.

9 April is Scotland's national unicorn day.

Above: Unicorn above carvings of Scottish monarchs surrounding the Mercat Cross.

Right: Unicorn on the Mercat Cross.

Union Street

Aberdeen's main street was hailed as one of the grandest streets in the whole of Europe, blending 'the architectural beauties of London west-end streets, with the gaiety and brilliancy of the Parisian atmosphere ... lofty, elegant houses, the beautifully-white, flowing muslin curtains in the first and second floor windows, the expanded shop fronts, set out with such a profusion of rich and costly wares ...'

In 1801 one of Europe's grandest thoroughfares sliced through and passed over the top of Aberdeen's medieval confusion of lanes, wynds and burns to ensure smoother access to the city from west and north (via its link with King Street), and of course, flaunt the city's wealth and confidence (albeit it went bankrupt as a result). Erecting the eastern end of the street over arches sometimes 50 feet above ground level was ambitious and eye-wateringly expensive. Twenty-one reliable Aberdonians were given responsibility for the street's financial arrangements with some monies being drawn from the Common Good Fund. The debts incurred were paid off relatively quickly, by 1825.

Left: Union Street narrows at Union Bridge. The Palace hotel is on the left and Monkey House on the right.

Below: Union Bridge with the Bow Brig behind.

Union Street slowly emerged in its familiar form. Housebuilding began on the south side between the Shiprow and Putachieside (Market Street) and over time the street became home to some of Scotland's finest architecture. The street with its pristine town houses must have fairly glinted in the sunshine for granite reflects light rather than absorbing it like other stone and brick. Two hundred years later its granite is dulled by decades of soot, smoke and general pollution, but though the shine has faded its grandeur remains.

This new street straddling the Denburn Valley was in need of a bridge. On 7 July 1801 the foundation stone of the imaginatively named Union Bridge was laid by Provost and Master of the Lodge of Aberdeen John Dingwall. Into the hollowed-out stone went a casket containing participants' names; a jar of coins; an inscription on vellum plus written copy; tables listing Aberdeen's customs, shore and weigh-house duties; a copy of *Aberdeen Journal* of 14 April 1800, which included mention of the parliament act that approved the city's new streets; a city almanac for 1801; and much else. Prayers were said, the Master Mason checked all was well with a Square, Level and Plumb, knocked the stone three times with a mallet to three cheers from spectators, the national anthem was played and the Infantry Volunteers fired a royal salute. Two years later, on 25 August 1803, the keystone in the 130-foot single-span bridge was installed with equal ceremony.

In the end the bridge proved unpopular with carters, cab and tram drivers forced to queue to pass where it narrowed from Union Street. The bridge was widened and today it is visible only on its northern side for the south parapet has been obliterated following more dubious planning decisions from the council.

Union Terrace

Union Terrace was transformed in 1878 from a narrow and inconsequential 5-foot-wide lane into a splendid 30-foot-broad thoroughfare with generous pavements. The east pavement was narrowed in 1931 to widen the road to ease traffic congestion.

Grand offices and banks along the west side of the terrace exuded the confidence of that time, but their imposing appearance has been somewhat undermined with subsequent modifications that have spoiled the integrity of the street.

The best statue on the terrace is the 1892 bronze of Robert Burns that has the poet striking a natural stance as though pausing mid-stride to chat to passers-by. Local sculptor Henry Bain Smith depicted him with a Tam o' Shanter in one hand and a daisy in the other (which some folk think can become their keepsake). This tribute to the people's poet was paid for by the people of Aberdeen.

The remaining two statues on the terrace indulged in a game of musical chairs when Edward VII was placed at the corner of Union Street, a position above the men's underground lavatory previously occupied by Prince Albert who moved his chair nearer to the library. Local opinion refused to sanction the uprooting of Burns in favour of Edward.

Union Terrace and the Trainie Park.

Union Terrace Gardens

Old trees, remnants of the Corbie Haugh where corbies (crows or rooks) nested, were felled to create a pleasure garden in 1879 between Union Terrace and the Great North of Scotland Railway, which gave its alternative name, Trainie Park. The promised bowling green never materialised; giant draughts did and were popular but later removed. Sculpture, too, has been largely absent from the park, perhaps because of the curious incident of the American soldier.

One day in 1893 Aberdonians awoke to find a statue of an armed American in the Trainie Park. A fault in its carving meant the granite sculpture could not be sold to

Above: A busy Union Terrace Gardens.

Left: Denburn Gardens, later Union Terrace Gardens, prior to the Viaduct.

its American buyer so the park's convenor took an executive decision to place it in the gardens, to the embarrassment of its granite manufacturer and bewilderment of many. A bemused park-keeper quipped it might be passed off as William Wallace's father (Wallace's statue stood nearby), however it was quickly removed.

Universities

Aberdeen has had two universities for most of the years since 1593: King's in Old Aberdeen, Marischal in new Aberdeen and latterly Robert Gordon University.

St Mary's College became Scotland's third university in 1495 when Bishop Elphinstone established courses in theology, canon and civil law, medicine and the liberal arts based on teaching at Paris and Orléans. St Mary's (of the Nativity) was soon renamed King's in honour of James IV – the first university in the British Isles to teach medicine with its appointment of a Mediciner in 1505.

Aberdeen's second university, Marischal College, was founded in 1593 at the Broadgate by George Keith, 5th Earl Marischal. It was modestly established with a principal, three professors, a steward, cook and six alumni (selected on grounds of poverty who paid their professors what they could afford and in return were obliged to waken everyone at 5 a.m.). These black-gowned and bonneted students did not study all the time but amused themselves shooting from butts outside Marischal until their reckless firing of arrows presented so much risk to townsfolk the practice was ended in the 1600s. A less disruptive pastime popular with students was football and new students, *bajans* later *bejans*, had to 'furnish foot-balls to the other classes', but unlike some universities there was no bullying or 'fagging' of young students at Marischal.

The difference between King's and Marischal was significant in religious terms: King's was associated with the 'old' religion, Catholicism, and Marischal with Protestantism. In 1689 an effigy of the Pope was tried, condemned and burnt by Marischal students at the Mercat Cross.

After 250 years as separate institutions, King's and Marischal merged in 1860 to become the University of Aberdeen following an Act of Parliament in 1858, 'for the better government and discipline of the Universities of Scotland' and improve educational standards in both. An earlier union contemplated by their principals in 1641 to create the King Charles' University failed.

Aberdeen University
sculpture with King's in
the background.

V

Vennel

This Scots word for narrow corridor comes from the French *la venelle* or narrow street. Aberdeen had many such closes, *flowers of Aberdeen*, and a couple were simply known as 'the vennel' where

> Vagrant lodgers –
> Wi' tinklers, knaves, pig-wives, and cadgers,
> The coarsest kin' o' Chelsea sodgers,
> Like beggars dress'd
> In holes an' dens, like toads an' badgers,
> Here make their nest.

A vennel clambering up St Katherine's hill from the Shiprow was just 5 feet wide, scarcely enough for two men to squeeze past each other or one loaded horse. A vennel that ran from the Gallowgate to the Loch was torn down in 1842.

Viaduct

Hilly Aberdeen city centre sits on a series of bridges or viaducts constructed to facilitate the town's expansion. Rosemount Viaduct, built in 1886–67 over the northern railway

Rosemount Viaduct.

and lower Denburn, afforded easy access between Schoolhill, Union Terrace and the suburb of Rosemount, and provided a site for the library, St Marks and HMT.

Victoria Bridge

Prior to the erection of Victoria Bridge at Torry, the Dee was crossed upriver at the Bridge of Dee, the Chain Briggie from 1830 or ferryboat. On 5 April 1876 holidaying Aberdonians heading for the Bay of Nigg packed onto the small ferry, which became unstable in the river swollen with snowmelt. It capsized with a loss of thirty-three lives. Pathetic accounts emerged of the drowned, their arms wrapped around one another and of a dead little boy still clutching the tuppence-ha'penny change from the fourpence his parents gave him for the fare. In light of this disaster the public paid for a five-arch bridge of Kemnay granite which has provided safe access between town and Torry since 2 July 1881.

Above: Victoria Bridge.

Right: The Chain Briggie from the Monkey Brae.

Wallace

The colossus of Aberdeen, this monumental statue of William Wallace on the Viaduct, the best figurative sculpture of the Guardian of Scotland in the country, is the work of Edinburgh sculptor William Grant Stevenson whose fellow townsman John Steill left a bequest of £3,000 for a statue to the Scottish hero with instructions it should be 'bold' and 'massive'. It certainly is. Steill's other instruction was it should show Wallace ordering the English foe at the Battle of Stirling Bridge to 'Go back to your masters and tell them that we came not here to treat but to fight and set Scotland free' – those words are cut into the rustic pink Corrennie granite plinth along with others associated with Wallace. He was betrayed, charged and convicted of being a traitor to the King of England. Sadistically killed, Wallace was stripped naked, chained to a horse and dragged through London, partially hanged, cut down at the point of death and his organs were torn from his body and burnt. Finally, Wallace's head and limbs were severed, his head displayed on a spike at London Bridge and his limbs distributed around the country to demonstrate the consequence of resistance to England. Some historians are quick to quash stories that Wallace's arm was sent to Aberdeen and kept at St Machar's Cathedral. Nevertheless, the lane around there is known as Wallace Wynd.

William Wallace, Guardian of Scotland.

Extract from
Wallace's address
to his troops on the
statue plinth.

"When I was a youth, and under the care of my uncle, all that I could carry away from him was a single proverb, but it seemed to me above all price, and I never forgot it. It was this:— 'I tell you a truth, liberty is the best of all things. My son, never live under any slavish bond!'"

Remarks by WALLACE on the instructions he received from his Uncle, the Priest of Dunipace. "I have brought you to the Ring — Dance according to your skill." WALLACE DREW UP HIS ARMY AT FALKIRK IN A CIRCULAR FORM AND ADDRESSED THEM AS ABOVE.

Wallace Tower

The sixteenth-century Z-plan tower house popularly known as the Wallace Tower because of the little soldier in a wall niche dubbed William Wallace stands on raised ground at Tillydrone. In its original form it occupied a position in the heart of Aberdeen at the Wallace neuk on the Netherkirkgate until relocated under pressure from Marks & Spencer who wanted to expand their store.

Witches

'Wise folk' who concocted remedies for ailments physical and mental from plants and animals exist today but are no longer burnt at the stake. Witch persecutions increased at times of peril such as plague or severe hardship – easy scapegoats to carry blame.

Janet Wishart and her family were victims of witch hysteria. One Halloween in 1596 a party in the Castlegate was sensationally reported as a 'witch dance' with *Satan* playing on his 'Instrumentis' and revellers dressed as hares and cats – animals linked to the supernatural. Thomas Leys, Janet's son, was Master of Ceremonies and he along with his parents and three sisters were tried as witches. His father and sisters were found partly guilty and banished from the town but Thomas and his mother were strangled and burnt at the stake.

'Swimming the witch' was another shameful practice employed when there was no evidence to convict someone but determination to persecute them. The accused, usually a woman, was dropped into the harbour. If she floated she was guilty and if she sank she was innocent – but by then, of course, she had drowned. Women were frequently *douket at the Cran* (crane), chained to the jib and submerged into the harbour for reasons other than witchcraft. After 1703 witchcraft was removed from the statute of criminal offences.

Wizard

The Great Wizard of the North was one of the world's greatest showmen. The Wizard, aka John Henry Anderson, aka Professor Anderson, orphaned aged ten, was apprenticed to a coachmaker, but John's imagination was fired by conjuring tricks he'd seen practised and one day he took off with a travelling company.

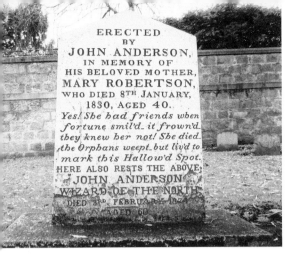

The Great Wizard of the North's gravestone.

John Anderson originated the rabbit-out-of-the-hat routine. He perfected sleight-of-hand tricks and breathtaking illusions such as catching a bullet fired from a gun, which helped place him among the world's most highly regarded entertainers. He was infused with magic and wonder. In a letter to the *Aberdeen Journal* he described his enchantment at seeing sharks and albatrosses and smelling icebergs on a voyage to Australia. In Australia he found nearly every other person was an Aberdonian and the very landscape reminded him of his north-east home.

For forty years the world was entertained and bamboozled by the Wizard of the North. When he died in February 1874 Anderson was buried alongside his beloved mother, Mary Robertson, in St Nicholas Kirkyard and his name added to the memorial stone he erected for her containing this melancholy inscription:

> Yes! She had friends when
> fortune smiled, if frown'd
> they knew her not! She died
> the orphan wept but lived to
> mark this Hallowed Spot.

That this showman's contribution to magic was recognised the world over was testified to by his obituary in the *New York Times* and in 1909 the Great Houdini paid homage to his hero when he visited the Wizard of the North's grave in Aberdeen.

Woolmanhill

Woolmanhill was possibly named after a wool market. Fleeces and wool were high-value products for export and local manufacturing. Until this century Aberdeen was a centre of woollen garment production, from stockings to haute couture fashions.

The animal grazing parks and bleach fields where crowds gathered to dance and watch miracle plays became the site of Aberdeen's first infirmary. In 1739 the burgesses of Aberdeen proposed a hospital to house and treat the town's sick and so in May 1742 Aberdeen got its first infirmary just outside the city centre.

X = Ten Stuart Monarchs on the Mercat Cross

Ten portraits of Stuart monarchs surround the Mercat Cross. Built in 1686 this cross, regarded as the best in Scotland, once stood on a raised platform on the Plainstones at the Tolbooth but moved to its present site in the Castlegate in 1842.

This delightful freestone hexagonal-arched cross replaced an earlier one 'of the more ancient Cross no description has been preserved, nor is the date of its foundation known, but from incidental notices we may conjecture that it differed little from the structure by which it was re-placed'.

The cross, sometimes open, sometimes enclosing little shops, sometime a post office, sometime a coach office and sometime adorned with iron railings, was the work of mason John Montgomery of Rayne and cost 800 merks. It is decorated with ten

Above left: The Mercat Cross and Record Office.

Above right: Engraving of the Mercat Cross and original unicorn.

Detail on the
Mercat Cross.

medallions of the Stuart monarchs, the Royal Arms (removed during the Cromwell government and later restored), the Burgh Arms, animal gargoyles which drain rainwater and a thistle-bound Corinthian column with unicorn emerging from its roof.

Mercat Crosses were the centre of civic life. When a monarch died, as in 1685 with Charles II's death, the cross (the earlier one) was draped with black cloth and town bells muffled. Mourning at Aberdeen Cross was fleeting, for next day the town awoke to a cacophony of bells, bonfires and a procession to the cross transformed with colourful embroidered panels to celebrate a new king. Toasts were offered, the cry 'God save the King, James VII' went out, and the following year the present Mercat Cross appeared with the face of James VII, making ten Stuarts in all from James I to James VII, Mary, Charles I and II.

There might have been eleven for on 20 September 1715 James VIII, dubbed the Old Pretender by his political and religious enemies, was declared king at the cross by the Earl Marischal but by then Catholic monarchs were proscribed in Britain, a decision which led to the Jacobite (followers of James) risings, so irrespective of Aberdeen's support he was never crowned.

In 1745 the anti-Jacobite Provost Morrison and officials pocketed the keys to the Mercat Cross and went into hiding just as Jacobites were about to declare support for James. When unearthed Morrison was forced to the cross at sword point but still refusing to toast him had wine poured down his throat. Shortly after government troops poured into Aberdeen determined to nip any residual Jacobite leanings in the bud.

Ringing of a handbell or bugle blast alerted townsfolk to declarations at the Mercat Cross; the last monarch proclaimed there was Victoria in 1837 before the cross lost its civic role. Public punishments at the cross also declined – branding with hot irons, whippings, the branks and pillories and, of course, executions.

The majority of Mercat Cross activities, however, were cheerful – 1,000 years of lively markets and fairs, roller-skating rinks and the annual demonstrations by Aberdeen's fire brigade on the eve of magistrate elections, which provided the cross and its ten monarchs with a good wash down: 'the ruff of the beautiful Mary' and her young son James would have his doublet scoured and anyone who got in the way of their hoses'.

Y

YCND

The menace of nuclear weapons and threat of the Cold War led to the formation of the Campaign for Nuclear Disarmament (CND) in the 1950s. In Aberdeen an offshoot youth movement, YCND formed in 1965 by young workers, students and school pupils, broadened their protests to include opposition to the Vietnam War. They met weekly in the Trades Hall at the Adelphi and this dynamic group, one of the biggest in Britain, produced magazines, leaflets, posters, whitewashed slogans on city centre streets, held marches along Union Street and vigils at King Edward's statue and the US military base at Edzell.

YCND anti-Vietnam War march along Union Street in 1965.

Z

Zanre

Zanre's West End Soda Fountain at No. 3 Rose Street was a home from home for Aberdeen's youth. One of several Italian cafés in the city, Zanre's Soda Fountain was a favourite. Their ices claimed many awards and happily for north-east ice cream lovers this area was judged top in the Ice Cream Alliance's best British ice cream awards of 1959 with the Soda Fountain scooping up prizes.

Zulu

Small sail fishing boats from Moray, zulus were once a familiar sight in Aberdeen Harbour unloading their catches of herring. A stronger Zulu connection with the city came when Hall, Russell's shipyard launched *Umvoti* and *Ingeli*. *Umvoti* was a three-masted iron barque whose name in Zulu means 'one who flows quietly'. Launched in 1869, she transported cargo between Mauritius and Western Australia including horses but more pertinently for a Zulu-named ship she transported troops during the Zulu war. *Ingeli* was a passenger steamship launched in 1897 and named after a mountain in Zululand.

The West End Soda Fountain.